# A Cup of Coffee

*From Plantation to Pot, A Coffee Lover's Guide to the Perfect Brew*

# A Cup of Coffee

### From Plantation to Pot, A Coffee Lover's Guide to the Perfect Brew

## Norman Kolpas

### Principal Photographer: Bill Milne

Grove Press   New York

A FRIEDMAN GROUP BOOK

Published in the United States by Grove Press
A division of Grove Press, Inc.
841 Broadway
New York, New York 10003-4793

ISBN 0-8021-1476-8

Library of Congress Cataloging-in-Publication Data

Kolpas, Norman.
A cup of coffee / Norman Kolpas.—1st ed.
p.  cm.
"A Friedman Group book"—T.p. verso.
Includes index.
ISBN 0-8021-1476-8
1. Coffee.  2. Coffee—History.  3. Coffee—Folklore.  I. Title.

TX817.C6K65  1993
641.3′373—dc20          91-38273
CIP

*A CUP OF COFFEE*
*From Plantation to Pot, a Coffee Lover's*
*Guide to the Perfect Brew*
was prepared and produced by
Michael Friedman Publishing Group, Inc.
15 West 26th Street
New York, New York 10010


Editor: Nathaniel Marunas
Art Director: Jeff Batzli
Designer: Stephanie Bart-Horvath
Photography Editor: Ede Rothaus


Typeset by Bookworks plus
Color separations by United South Seas Graphic Art Co., Ltd.
Printed and bound in Hong Kong by Leefung-Asco Printers Ltd.

First Edition 1993
10 9 8 7 6 5 4 3 2 1

All flag illustrations © The Flag Research Center, Winchester, Massachusetts

*For Katie,*
*the best person I know*
*to share a cup of coffee with.*

My sincerest thanks to Karla Olson, who first suggested the project to me, and to Nathaniel Marunas, who saw the manuscript through its editing, design, and production with both tact and aplomb. Kudos to Ede Rothaus, who performed her usual miracle of photo and illustration research and acquisition, and Stephanie Bart-Horvath, who provided the exquisite design one expects from Friedman Publishing. Lastly, thanks as always to Michael Friedman for his friendship and support.

# CONTENTS

*In Budapest, a porcelain espresso machine charmingly evokes the turn of the century, when Hungarian coffeehouses flourished with social and cultural life.*

# INTRODUCTION

*M*ore than one third of the world's people drink coffee today. And, impressive though that figure alone may be, it conceals a far more interesting array of facts.

Coffee's popularity is not confined to any one country, continent, or culture. It is found in the Middle East, where the coffee habit originated and where the way in which the drink is enjoyed has changed little in hundreds of years. It is drunk in Africa, where modern coffee cultivation and commerce coexist with ancient customs. In Europe, the coffeehouse still reigns as a social hub, and the *Kaffeeklatsch* as a high form of social art. In the United States, one of the highest forms of praise one can bestow upon a dining establishment or a host or hostess is that they serve "a good cup of coffee." In Latin America, this prime commodity has not surprisingly become an integral part of daily life. Even in parts of Asia, a region of the world generally characterized as tea-totalling, coffee's popularity is firmly entrenched or rapidly growing.

Coffee habits, in turn, are as varied as the nations in which the beverage is enjoyed. The coffee beans may be lightly toasted or roasted until almost burnt; ground coarsely or to a fine powder; kept entirely pure, blended with other beans, or mixed with additives or flavorings. Brewed in a variety of ways, it may be sipped black, with a dash or flood of milk, or a dollop of whipped cream—it is enjoyed upon waking, in the late morning or at midday, as an afternoon ritual, an after-dinner flourish, or as a nightcap.

Everyone who loves the drink has his or her own coffee history to relate. I myself grew up in a family of tea drinkers, and my first experience with coffee was a fairly ordinary one—I drank cup after cup of milky, sweet stuff on an airplane flying home from final exams after my freshman year of college. Then there was a friend whose family were coffee connoisseurs so devoted to the brew in its purest form that milk and sugar were banished from its presence; with her, I learned the pleasures of grinding and brewing it fresh, and savoring it black. Travels in Europe and seven years living in London—where excellent purveyors of freshly roasted coffee may still be found—expanded the horizons of its appreciation even more for me. Back home in Los Angeles, I wooed my wife-to-be in part by freshly roasting coffee for her; today, our

*With its streetside tables and sweet specialties, a San Francisco cafe maintains its links to the coffeehouse traditions of the city's Italian settlers.*

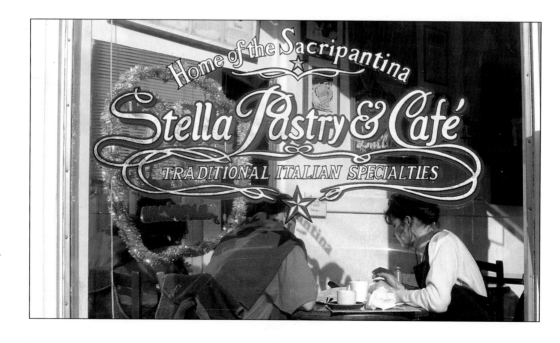

*Bags of beans from the world's coffee-growing countries, along with the paraphernalia with which the beans are brewed, crowd a coffee store in Charleston, South Carolina.*

little son makes pretend coffee every morning with his toy pots and pans. Every phase of my life seems linked, in some way, to coffee.

This book offers many different pathways by which you can enrich your own personal enjoyment of the brew. It begins with a history of coffee—surveying the legends, lore, and facts surrounding the discovery and worldwide spread of its appreciation and cultivation. It then explains how coffee grows, gets processed, comes to market, and finds its way into your kitchen, and continues with a comprehensive guide to selecting and preparing coffee. Such basics having been covered, the book goes on to explore the different ways in which cultures in the old and new worlds enjoy the brew, and offers suggestions—along with recipes—for ways in which you can use such customs when you entertain at home. The final chapter offers some simple guidelines for setting the coffee table and expanding your enjoyment through coffee collectibles. The appendix offers a quick reference source of further information about coffee and purveyors who offer good, quality beans.

There are many different ways to make use of *A Cup of Coffee*: as a practical reference; as a cookbook; and simply as a volume to be read and enjoyed. By all means, be sure to employ it in one very important way: as a coffee-table book, displayed for the appreciation of anyone who might partake of the brew in your company.

# HISTORY & TRADITION

**C**offee's worldwide history and the traditions and lore that have grown around it
are as rich, complex, and beguiling as the beverage itself. Coffee instilled near-
religious ecstasy in its earliest aficionados, and it incurred the wrath of zealots. It
has inspired flights of great artistry, and stirred political intrigue and revolt. Considered in turns cure-all and devil's brew, the drink of Everyman and the liquor of the
elite, an object of disdain and a cause for celebration, coffee has never failed to
elicit one emotion that perhaps best explains its powerful impact:
passion.

# Coffee in African & Middle Eastern Lore

Legend has it that an Abyssinian goatherd named Kaldi was the first to discover coffee more than a thousand years ago, when he noticed that his goats danced with glee after nibbling bright red berries growing on glossy green trees that were also decked with jasmine-scented blossoms. Kaldi tried the berries himself and was suddenly filled with energy and alertness. But when he brought the berries to a holy man, they were dismissed as devilish and thrown into the fire—from which they gave forth an enticing aroma. Quickly, the roasted beans were raked from the embers, ground up, and dissolved in hot water, yielding the world's first cup of coffee.

Fact, though not as romantic as legend, is no less interesting. The nomadic mountain warriors of the Galla tribe in Ethiopia may well have been the first to recognize coffee's energizing, sustaining effect—though not as a beverage. They gathered coffee beans from trees that grew in the wild, ground them up, and mixed them with animal fat, forming small balls that they carried as rations. Other tribes of northeastern Africa ate the beans as a porridge or drank a wine fermented from its fruit.

Sometime around the end of the first millennium A.D., Arab traders brought coffee back to their homeland. There the wild plant was cultivated for the first time on plantations, and two drinks known by the general term *kahwah* gradually came into favor: one, a tealike beverage called *kisher*, steeped from the fruit's husks; the other, *bounya*, a thick brew of ground beans.

So, although the coffee tree was not native to the Middle East, that region earned its reputation as the birthplace of coffee as we know it in the West. No single, definitive account exists of the drink's arrival or its rise to popularity. But numerous references can be found in scientific literature, folklore, and religious history.

The eleventh-century physician and philosopher Avicenna, for example, wrote that the drink "fortifies the members, cleans the skin, dries up the humidities that are under it, and gives an excellent smell to all the body." An Islamic man of medicine noted that "it is by experience found to conduce the drying of colds, persistent coughs and catarrh, and to unblock constipation and provoke urination; it allays high blood pressure, and is good against smallpox and measles"—appending the cautionary note that adding milk to the brew "may bring one in danger of leprosy."

Not surprisingly, legends arose ascribing a local origin to the beans and the beverage. Among the most poetic is the tale of Sheikh Omar, who was led by the spirit of his departed holy master, Abou'l Hasan Schadheli, to the port of Mocha, where he became a holy recluse living beside a spring surrounded by bright green bushes. The berries of those bushes sustained him, and he used them to cure the townspeople of a plague. Thus did coffee gain him the reputation of a great sage, healer, and holy man.

By the sixteenth century, coffee drinking was widespread in the Arab world—even in the holy city of Mecca, where it had been brought by Yemeni dervishes who drank it during their strenuous ceremonies of worship. Throughout the city, as elsewhere, people gathered to play

*Starting in the seventeenth century, Europeans of high social bearing, good taste, and learning came to appreciate the pleasures of a freshly brewed cup of coffee (page 12).*

*"Avoid the imitators," cautions a 1921 poster (left) for Cafe Martin, with a giddy measure of joie de vivre that has always characterized the French love of coffee.*

*An 1878 engraving (opposite page, top) shows bagged coffee receiving one more inspection from a foreman before being stacked in a plantation warehouse.*

*In this detail from an 1889 drawing by C.S. Reinhart, originally conceived to accompany a story by Sarah Orne Jewett, one character serves another his afternoon coffee.*

chess and other games, trade news and gossip, and sip coffee.

But opposition to coffee grew, fueled largely by those who saw a threat in the free speech that coffeehouses fostered. In 1511, Khair Beg, Mecca's corrupt governor, attempted to ban the drink, fearing that it might foster public opposition to his rule. In collaboration with his confessor, Shems-eddin, he put coffee on trial, summoning experts from every walk of life to testify against it. He issued a decree forbidding its public and private sale and consumption, but the decree stood only briefly, until the Cairo-based sultan of Egypt, his coffee-loving superior, revoked it. Just a year after banning coffee, Khair Beg's wrongdoings were uncovered, and he was executed.

The people of the Arab world felt strongly about their coffee—so much so that the export of green beans, from which plants could be grown, was completely banned. But roasted beans, and the drink brewed from them, gradually made their way beyond the Middle East, exciting a growing thirst for coffee in other countries.

# The Rise of the European Coffeehouse

European travelers to the Middle East were beguiled by the brew they enjoyed there: "a very good drink they call *Chaube* that is almost as black as ink and very good in illness, especially of the stomach," wrote the German physician and botanist Leonhard Rauwolf in 1582, in the first Western account of coffee. "This they drink in the morning early in open places before everybody, without any fear or regard, out of clay or China cups, as hot as they can, sipping it a little at a time."

By the early seventeenth century, coffee drinking had made sufficient inroads into the continent to stir attention in the highest of places. In Italy, Pope Clement VIII, faced with the rising power of the Ottoman Empire, was forced by his advisors to consider the favorite brew of Islamic lands as part of the infidel threat. One sip, however, and he decided instead to baptize the drink, making it an acceptable Christian beverage.

By 1645, the first coffeehouse had opened in Italy, and less than a hundred years later they were widespread throughout the country. Most celebrated were the cafes of Venice, particularly Caffe Florian, which was opened in 1720 by Floriono Francesconi, a friend of the celebrated sculptor Canova. As W. Carew Hazlitt wrote in *The Vene-*

### In Praise of Coffee

OH COFFEE, YOU DISPEL THE WORRIES OF THE GREAT, you point the way to those who have wandered from the path of knowledge. Coffee is the drink of the friends of God, and of His servants who seek wisdom.

As coffee steeps in the cup it gives off a musky aroma and turns the color of ink. No one can understand the truth until he drinks of its frothy goodness. Those who condemn coffee as causing man harm are fools in the eyes of God.

Coffee is the common man's gold, and like gold it brings to every man the feeling of luxury and nobility. Coffee differs from pure, gentle milk only in its taste and color. Take time in your preparation of coffee and God will be with you and bless you and your table. Where coffee is served there is grace and splendor and friendship and happiness.

All cares vanish as the coffee cup is raised to the lips. Coffee flows through your body as freely as your life's blood, refreshing all that it touches: look you at the youth and vigor of those who drink it.

Whoever tastes coffee will forever forswear the liquor of the grape. Oh drink of God's glory, your purity brings to man only well being and nobility.
—Sheikh Ansari Djezeri Hanball Abd-al-Kadir,
1587

*tian Republic*, "no establishment in Europe ever acquired such worldwide celebrity as that kept by Florian, the friend of Canova, and the trusted agent and acquaintance of hundreds of persons in and out of the city. . . . Venetian coffee was said to surpass all other, and the article placed before his visitors by Florian was said to be the best in Venice." Another friend, Carlo Goldoni, immortalized the establishment in his comic play, *The Coffee-House*. To this day, Caffe Florian thrives in St. Mark's Square.

Coffee took the *haute* road into French society. "A Turkish ambassador at Paris made the beverage highly fashionable," wrote Isaac D'Israeli. "The elegance of the equipage recommended it to the eye, and charmed the women: the brilliant porcelain cups, in which it was poured; the napkins fringed with gold, and the Turkish slaves on their knees presenting it to the ladies, seated on cushions, turned the heads of the Parisian dames." Soon street vendors were offering cups of fresh-brewed coffee door-to-door in Paris. And in 1686, a Florentine named Procopio dei Coltelli opened the still-surviving Cafe Procope, "a superior establishment," observed D'Israeli, "where literary men, artists, and wits resorted, to inhale the fresh and fragrant steam."

The Turks brought coffee to Austria in a less hospitable fashion. Their army surrounded Vienna in 1683, laying siege to the city. One Viennese citizen, a Pole named Franz George Kolschitzky, had lived in Turkey for some time, and slipped through the enemy lines in disguise to lead relief forces to the city. The Turks fled, leaving behind five hundred sacks of a "dry, black fodder" that Kolschitzky recognized as coffee—and claimed as his reward. He opened Vienna's first coffeehouse and established the habit of refining the brew by filtering out its grounds,

sweetening it, and adding a dash of milk.

The Netherlands' introduction to coffee held no high drama: by the early seventeenth century, Dutch traders had recognized the commodity's commercial appeal, and by the century's end had established plantations in Java with coffee plants smuggled from Arabia. But their introduction of the drink to Scandinavia met with governmental resistance, leading in 1756 to a short-lived Swedish ban

on coffee drinking. Even more insidious was Frederick the Great's attempt in 1767 to control the coffee habit and trade in Prussia, where more money was being spent on imported beans than on domestic beer. "Many battles have been fought and won by soldiers nourished on beer," his edict rationalized, "and the King does not believe that coffee-drinking soldiers can be depended upon . . . ." His tax officers, charged to sniff out contraband beans, came

*An orator holds forth in a British coffeehouse (previous page), gaining the attention of only some of its patrons. Men of wit and culture such as Pope, Bacon, Johnson, Boswell, Defoe, and Hogarth were patrons of such establishments.*

*As a favorite beverage, a social institution, and a cash crop, coffee gradually colonized the globe (right).*

to be known as "coffee smellers." Needless to say, the public's desire for coffee won in the end.

Surprisingly, for a nation whose image is so inextricably intertwined with tea, England took to coffee most wholeheartedly. In Oxford in 1650, a Mr. Jacobs opened the nation's first coffeehouse. London saw its first two years later, when a Greek named Pasqua Rosee, in collaboration with an Englishman named Daniel Edwards, opened a coffeehouse "in a shed in the churchyard in St. Michael, Cornhill." By 1700, more than two thousand such establishments could be found in the city—this despite King Charles II's proclamation of their abolition on January 10, 1676. This move was so vehemently opposed that it was appealed two days *before* its implementation.

This is not to say that coffee enjoyed entirely smooth sailing in Britain. With that nation's distinctive love of written discourse and debate, a war of pamphlets raged for and against coffeehouses. "The room stinks of tobacco worse than hell of brimstone," ranted one such disclaimer, published in 1673, "and is as full of smoke as their heads that frequent it, whose humours are as various as those of Bedlam, and their discourse oftentimes as heathenish, and dull as their liquor, which, by its looks and taste, you may reasonably guess to be Pluto's diet drink, that witches tipple out of dead men's skulls, when they ratify to Belzebub their sacramental vows." Rebutted a coffee lover: "a well-regulated coffee-house . . . is the sanctuary of health, the nursery of temperance, the delight of frugality, an academy of civility, and free-school of ingenuity." Such English cultural luminaries as Alexander Pope, Sir Francis Bacon, Samuel Johnson, James Boswell, Daniel Defoe, Sir Joshua Reynolds, Adam Smith, William Hogarth, Oliver Goldsmith, and Henry Fielding—coffeehouse habitués all—no doubt agreed with the latter argument. So entrenched did the coffeehouse become as an English social institution that such famed establishments as The Royal Society and Lloyd's of London began as places to enjoy the steaming brew.

Indeed, the role of the English coffeehouse as a bastion of free speech had far-reaching implications. For that English institution naturally found its way to the colonies in North America, where coffee and the places that served it played an integral role in the founding of a new nation.

# America's Coffee Revolution

European settlers no doubt brought coffee with them to the North American colonies throughout the seventeenth century. Within four years of Britain's gaining control of Dutch New Amsterdam in 1664, coffee had replaced beer as New York's favorite breakfast-time drink. William Penn was heard to gripe in 1683 that on a visit to that city he paid an exorbitant $4.68 per pound for unroasted coffee beans.

Throughout the colonies, coffeehouses gradually became social and political centers. A woman named Dorothy Jones received Boston's first license to sell coffee in 1670, but no record exists that she ever opened an establishment, suggesting instead that she may have sold ground coffee—known then as "coffee powder"—for home consumption. The city's first place to gather over a steaming cup was the London Coffee House, opened in 1689. But the Green Dragon, founded eight years later, holds the distinction of being dubbed "headquarters of

the Revolution" by Daniel Webster. Here Paul Revere, John Adams, and other patriots reputedly planned the Boston Tea Party; they revolted against Britain's tax on tea by dumping a shipment of the stuff into Boston Harbor, thereby elevating coffee to the position of patriotic brew. Still another local coffeehouse, the Bunch of Grapes, was the stage for the first public reading of the Declaration of Independence.

New York had its own coffee-scented cradle of liberty in the Merchants Coffee House, at the southeast corner of Wall and Water streets. On April 18, 1774, the Sons of Liberty met there to turn away a shipment of tea carried by the British ship *Nancy*, commanded by Captain Lockyer. A month later, leading citizens convened there to draft a letter calling for a "virtuous and spirited Union" of the colonies, and a congress of deputies from each—the First Continental Congress. After the Revolution, the coffeehouse hosted still more historic events—including a grand reception thrown by the city's mayor and the state's governor on April 23, 1789, in honor of president-elect George Washington. Though the establishment burned to the ground in 1804, a plaque unveiled in 1914 commemorates its significant role in the nation's early years.

Long after the American Revolution, coffee continued to be the country's drink of choice, offering solace to hardworking settlers pushing ever further westward. During the Mexican-American War and the Civil War, coffee was an essential part of military rations, and its brewing was the high point of a soldier's weary day, according to Union veteran John D. Billings in his book *Hardtack and Coffee*: "The little campfires, rapidly increasing to hundreds in number, would shoot up along the hills and plains, and as if by magic, acres of territory would be lumi-

*A 1910 American illustration captures the warm camaraderie that could develop in any institution that offered good coffee and plenty of it.*

*Slender young coffee trees grow in dense profusion on a plantation set in the foothills of Costa Rica.*

nous with them. Soon they would be surrounded by the soldiers, who made it an invariable rule to cook their coffee first."

So far had American coffee come from its transatlantic origins that no less an authority than Mark Twain would look with disdain upon the beverage offered him in *A Tramp Abroad*: ". . . in Europe, coffee is an unknown beverage. You can get what the European hotel keeper thinks is coffee, but it resembles the real thing as hypocrisy resembles holiness. It is a feeble, characterless, uninspiring sort of stuff, and almost as undrinkable as if it had been made in an American hotel. . . . After a few months' acquaintance with European 'coffee,' one's mind weakens, and his faith with it, and he begins to wonder if the rich beverage of home, with its clotted layer of yellow cream on top of it, is not a mere dream after all, and a thing which never existed."

## Coffee Conquers Latin America & the Caribbean

Today—thanks to an ubiquitous Colombian advertisement featuring a smiling coffee grower and his packmule, and the near-legendary status of beans from a Jamaican region known as Blue Mountain—it is all too easy to think of coffee as being indigenous to Latin America and the Caribbean. But less than three centuries ago, the growing, processing, and brewing of coffee was unknown in this part of the world.

That situation changed largely through the heroic efforts of one man: Gabriel Mathieu de Clieu. A captain of

25

*Rakes in hand, plantation workers spread just-picked coffee berries in the sun to ferment and dry in the method known as dry curing.*

infantry in the Caribbean colony of Martinique, de Clieu recognized the potential of coffee cultivation in the New World—even though French government attempts to start plantations in the Antilles had failed. On home leave in Paris in 1723, the thirty-five-year-old officer used his relationship with a lady in the French court to join in league with the royal physician and sneak under cover of darkness into the Jardin des Plantes, where they stole three seedlings from a coffee tree that had been presented by the burgomaster of Amsterdam to King Louis IV.

Embarking from Nantes, de Clieu and the coffee trees endured attacks by Tunisian pirates and a violent ocean storm. But a calm slowed the voyage and led to water rationing. Two of his tiny charges died, and de Clieu kept the third alive only by sharing his water rations with it.

In Martinique, de Clieu planted the survivor in his garden, hidden by thorn bushes. Four years later, de Clieu recalled, "I gathered about two pounds of seed which I distributed among all those whom I thought most capable of giving the plants the care necessary for their prosperity." Within fifty years, an official survey recorded almost nineteen million coffee trees growing on the island. This gave rise to many plantations elsewhere in the New World, while also serving the ever-growing coffee habit of Europe. Martinique coffee, "plain, spicy, nourishing as well as stimulating," wrote the French historian Michelet, "fed the adulthood of the century. . . ; it added its fervor to fervent souls, its light to the penetrating sight of the prophets gathered in the 'den of Procope' who saw at the bottom of the black brew the ray of the revolution to come."

Around the same time as de Clieu's venture, other plantations were begun in colonies in the Caribbean and Latin America. The huge Brazilian coffee industry had its start with the romantic escapade of Lieutenant Colonel Francisco de Melo Palheta, who was sent by his government in 1727 to arbitrate a border dispute between the nearby French and Dutch colonies in the Guianas. He settled the dispute as easily as he charmed the wife of French Guiana's governor, with whom he struck up a secret liaison. Although France jealously guarded its coffee plantations to prevent cultivation from spreading in the New World, the lady bade farewell to Palheta with a bouquet in which she hid cuttings and fertile seeds of coffee—the first to be planted in Brazil.

Today, Brazil supplies the world with roughly a third of its coffee. And Brazilians may well be Latin America's greatest coffee drinkers: in the average day, a serious lover of coffee there may consume between twenty and forty small cups of *cafezhino* per day.

# The Modern Coffee Renaissance

The coffee habit has never seemed in danger of extinction. Indeed, coffee appears to hold more appeal today for the informed consumer than ever before, for a variety of reasons.

Faced with growing concern, for example, over the effects of caffeine—the stimulant present in coffee—the coffee industry responded with ever more effective and safe methods for decaffeinating coffee without impairing its flavor. Today, it is possible to enjoy excellent-tasting coffee—even after-dinner espresso—from which 97 percent or more of the caffeine has been removed.

Furthermore, coffee has benefited from the growing gourmet revolution that has swept the world since the 1970s. Just as people who have learned to prepare and enjoy the finest in food and drink have come to know the ins and outs of international and ethnic cuisines, fresh produce, and boutique wines, so has their interest continued to grow in what are known as specialty coffees—freshly roasted, high-quality varieties or blends specifically selected by the consumer, purchased freshly ground or as whole beans, to be carefully prepared at home using a preferred type of brewing equipment. Since 1980, specialty coffees in America have exhibited a 15 percent growth in sales each year.

Perhaps this increased awareness of the depths of pleasure to be gained from savoring good coffee has led to yet another significant phenomenon as the twentieth century draws to a close: the return of the coffeehouse. In large cities and small towns, in the New World and the Old, business establishments specializing in brewing and serving coffee have once again become favored gathering spots for young and old alike. Some seem to take their cue from a century or more ago, offering a genteel, wood-panelled atmosphere complete with racks of magazines and daily newspapers for patrons to study. Others hark back to the "beatnik" coffeehouses of the 1950s—student hangouts complete with thrift-shop furnishings, mismatched china, rough-and-ready art on the walls, and folk music several nights a week. Still others look to the future, serving up excellent brew in high-tech ambience.

Times and styles may indeed change. But coffee—aromatic, rich, warming, sustaining, and brimming with inspiration—endures.

*A drive-up espresso stand in a parking lot shows just how readily coffee has adapted to the modern commuter age.*

# FROM PLANTATION TO COFFEE POT

Seldom do we stop in the course of our lives to wonder precisely from where those things upon which we rely each day come. Next time you sip a cup of coffee, muse upon some of the remarkable details of its trip from far-off plantation to your local coffee store. Use the insights on the following pages to lead you to better-informed decisions on the kinds of coffee you buy and to ways of preparation that will help you savor every last iota of wonderful flavor.

# Coffee Cultivation

The coffee tree is as remarkable to behold as the beverage its bean yields is wonderful to drink. Slender and somewhat pyramid-like in shape, the evergreen can grow some ten to twenty feet (3–6m) or more high. Its leaves, arrayed in pairs along the branches, are slender and lance-shaped, with a bright, waxy sheen. The blossoms, delicate and white, smell so intensely of jasmine that on some coastal plantations their scent wafts as far as three miles (4.8km) out to sea. Small, cherrylike berries, which develop at the same time other parts of a branch may be in blossom, ripen to a deep red; at their centers, enshrouded in a tough parchment-like covering, are pairs of seeds—the coffee beans.

The species of tree known as *Coffea arabica*, after its region of origin, is the source of the world's finest-tasting, most drinkable coffee. Scores of other related species exist. Most notable is *Coffea robusta*, a hearty species that matures more quickly than *arabica* and costs less to grow, making it an attractive crop for poorer coffee-producing countries; its beans have far less subtlety, though, and are used primarily in commercial blends as a background for finer-tasting coffees. Other species include *liberica, cattura,* and *excelsa.*

Coffee trees thrive in a globe-encircling geographic region known as the "coffee belt," between latitude 25 degrees north and latitude 30 degrees south, which covers numerous countries in central and western Africa, the Middle East, India, Southeast Asia and the Pacific, Latin America, and the Caribbean. Within this belt, the ideal growing conditions are found in mid-mountain forests with tall trees that cool and filter the two hours of direct sunshine coffee requires each day. Abundant, year-long rainfall; rich, well-drained volcanic soil; and year-round temperatures of around 70 degrees Fahrenheit (21°C) all contribute to the trees' peak performance. As with the grapes that are used to make a fine wine, each of these factors—altitude, sunshine, rain, soil, and temperature—along with how the beans are harvested and processed, affects the characteristics of the beverage you drink.

*In Guatemala, coffee fields climb the slopes of the San Pedro volcano, benefiting from the site's well-drained volcanic soil.*

Campesinos *on a Honduran coffee plantation load young trees onto pack animals (page 28) for transport to the field for planting.*

*Coffee trees bursting into flower. A tree may have blossoms, green berries, and fully ripe red fruit all at the same time.*

*Coffee trees thrive on a plantation near the rainforest at Buon Ma Thuot in the central highlands of Vietnam.*

Today's coffee plantations range from small, peasant-owned farms to immense corporate estates of a million trees or more. Regardless of its scale, however, each coffee-growing effort begins with select coffee seeds from prime specimens, stripped of their skins and pulp and planted in nursery beds. When the seedlings are a few months old and several inches high, they are transplanted to individual pots or bags of soil, where they continue to grow until they are about one year old and one and a half to two feet (0.5–0.7m) tall. Finally, the young trees are planted in rows about ten feet (3m) apart, interspersed with fast-growing shade trees.

Within three to five years, the trees—normally pruned to a six-foot (2m) height for ease of harvesting—reach fruit-bearing age; they achieve their most abundant maturity somewhere around their early teens, and can be expected to survive up to forty years or as long as a century. Their blossoms, which last but a few days, give way to green berries that ripen to cherry red in six months. In a single year, a good tree will yield up to twelve pounds (5.4kg) of fruit, which, after processing, become four to five pounds (1.8–2.2kg) of ready-to-roast beans.

## Grow Your Own Coffee Tree

THOUGH YOU SHOULDN'T EXPECT to get a decent crop of beans or cup of coffee from it, a coffee tree can make an attractive ornamental houseplant. You may find young trees in some quality nurseries, or fertile coffee seeds can sometimes be purchased through seed catalogs. (Green, unroasted coffee beans from a store are unlikely to germinate.)

If you buy seeds, plant them in the spring in sterile potting sand, no more than about one half inch (1.3cm) below the surface. Keep the sand damp, warm, and away from direct sunlight; cover with glass or plastic wrap to simulate a greenhouse and speed germination. When shoots appear, uncover the plant and move it to a semi-shaded spot. Once the seedlings are about four inches (10cm) tall, transplant to individual pots containing a potting mixture composed of equal parts loam, sand, and peat moss.

Keep the soil moist—but not overly so—during warm months, and spray the leaves daily with a mister. Feed monthly with a lime-free fertilizer. In cold months, keep the plant at comfortable room temperature and water less frequently, keeping the soil only slightly damp to the touch; feed lightly every other month.

Indoor coffee trees will generally reach a height of about three feet (1m), and in summer will display fragrant white blossoms—if not a tiny harvest of coffee berries.

# Harvesting, Curing, & Grading Coffee

Growing coffee, painstaking and time-consuming though it may be, is only the beginning of the beverage's trip to your cup. At the moment the coffee berry is ripe for the picking, it has yet to go through a number of critical stages, each of which will have an effect on the brew ultimately produced by the beans at its heart.

First among these stages is the harvesting. Since any branch of a coffee tree may simultaneously contain blossoms, both young-green and just-ripening fruit, and fully ripe coffee berries, careful handpicking is called for, as frequently as once every one to two weeks. If the beans are harvested too early, their flavor will not be fully matured, while late harvesting of overripe fruit can yield beans whose flavor will be tainted. The best plantations take meticulous care, while producers of lesser-quality coffees may sweep through the plantation stripping all fruit—green, ripe, and overripe—from the trees. On a good day, a plantation worker picking by hand can reap up to two hundred pounds (91kg) of ripe coffee berries, which will ultimately become about fifty pounds (23kg) of ready-to-

*Taller trees provide shade and shelter for young coffee trees on a plantation in Puriscal, Costa Rica (opposite page).*

*On a plantation near São Paulo, Brazil, a worker picks coffee by hand (left)—ensuring that only perfectly ripe fruit is removed from the tree.*

35

roast beans through one of two basic processing methods: dry curing and wet curing.

Dry curing is the more primitive method, and is still used for more than three fifths of the world's coffee. As the name suggests, the coffee berries are spread to dry in open sunshine and raked and respread several times a day. At night, they are raked into piles and covered for protection against moisture. Within two to three weeks, the fruit is completely dry and ready to be stripped by a hulling machine.

The wet method—far more mechanized—begins with a depulping machine that strips away the fruity pulp from the coffee berries, leaving their sticky centers enwrapping parchment-shielded beans. These are sluiced in large tanks for twelve to twenty-four hours, which causes them to ferment slightly, loosening the beans' coverings and incidentally developing their flavor. Finally, the last of the pulp and the parchment are washed away in sluiceways with continuously running water, leaving behind naked beans that are dried in the sun or in machines. Finally, a hulling machine removes the last bits of protective covering from the green beans.

Because every step of a coffee crop's preparation—from the selection of the plantation setting to the attention given the growing trees, from the care taken in harvesting through the curing method used—has an effect on the finished product, coffee beans are as a rule carefully graded for quality. Grading takes place on-site at large plantations, or at exporters' warehouses for smaller growing operations.

First, sorting machines feed the beans through a series of screens, each one punctuated by holes slightly bigger than the preceding screen, until all the beans—smallest to

largest—drop through. Each sized lot is then further graded by weight. Hand sorting, sometimes called "European preparation," may also be applied to remove any foreign objects or imperfect beans.

Cuptesting—the actual roasting, grinding, and brewing of a small sample of each batch of coffee (see page 38)—is the final test applied. Based upon this test, along with information on the coffee's source and curing method and the beans' physical characteristics, the coffee is given a rating that indicates its quality for purposes of pricing and sale. Different coffee-producing countries establish their own criteria and designations. Colombia's best beans, for example, are labelled "Supremo"; next comes "Excelso," the only other grade deemed worthy of export. These are followed by such grades as "Extra" and "Pasilla" (the lowest grade). Kenya's coffees get school-like grades of A, B, and C, with AA reserved for the best of all. Costa Rica's grades are, in descending order, Strictly Hard Bean, Good Hard Bean, Hard Bean, Medium Hard Bean, High Grown Atlantic, Medium Grown Atlantic, and Low Grown Atlantic.

Such grades affect the price at which the coffee will be sold to the exporter, the importer or broker, the retailer, and ultimately the consumer. Grading also serves as some indication of the quality of the coffee.

*Following the dry curing method still practiced on some plantations, harvested beans on a Vietnamese plantation are spread along a roadside.*

# Cuptesting

Coffee's most exacting rite of passage is known as "cup-testing," "cuptasting," or just plain "cupping." Whichever term is used, each succinctly describes the act of assessing, for commercial purposes, the qualities of a particular batch of beans by freshly roasting, brewing, and tasting it.

This is work for serious and talented professionals, who may work for a national coffee board, an exporter or importer, or a commercial coffee-selling enterprise. "A cuptaster has not only got to have a good tongue and nose, but a good mouth and good health as well," wrote V. Balu in the journal *India Coffee*. "He has got to maintain his tongue and nose in perfect order and keep the taste buds

of his tongue always in form. Above all, he has to be a strict disciplinarian and something of an ascetic." Helena Correa G., writing for the newspaper *El Tiempo* in Bogota, noted some of the special rules by which the twelve men and women who serve as Colombia's official tasters—*catadores*—must live: a maximum age of thirty-six years, with a career averaging eight years; "no smoking, no eating of spicy or greasy food, no drinking of alcoholic beverages, no staying up late, and no gastric problems."

Such self-discipline serves to sharpen the senses of experts who have already demonstrated acute sensitivity to the fine points of coffee's aroma, flavor, and body, and have painstakingly learned to judge the drink with the utmost discernment. Equipped with a well-developed, complex vocabulary of tasting terms (see page 40), they spend every working day assessing as many as one hundred different lots of coffee.

Wherever cuptasting is performed, the same basic procedure is followed—one that the home coffee connoisseur can duplicate with simple equipment as an exercise in learning more about the beverage.

First, a small lot of green coffee beans is roasted to a fairly light color—just until its inherent aroma and flavor have developed, but before any of them might be masked by the chemical changes that occur in darker roasting.

Next, one tablespoon (15ml) of the coffee is coarsely ground and put into a six-ounce (19ml), nonreactive, porcelain or glass cup, which is then filled with fresh water that has been brought to just below the boiling point—210 degrees Fahrenheit (99°C).

After the coffee steeps for a couple of minutes, the nose is brought close to the cup for a first impression of the aroma as the crust of grounds floating on the surface is

---

## Coffee at Gunpoint

"THE COFFEE-MAKER WAS ALMOST READY to bubble. I turned the flame low and watched the water rise. It hung a little at the bottom of the glass tube. I turned the flame up just enough to get it over the hump and then turned it low again quickly. I stirred the coffee and covered it. I set my timer for three minutes. Very methodical guy, Marlowe. Nothing must interfere with his coffee technique. Not even a gun in the hand of a desperate character."

—Raymond Chandler,
*The Long Goodbye*

*A woman of the Kikuyu tribe hand-picks ripe coffee berries on a plantation in the highlands north of Nairobi, Kenya.*

broken with a metal tasting spoon the size of a soup spoon. When the grounds have settled, a spoonful of the brew is swiftly sucked up through pursed lips, swished around the mouth so it coats all the taste buds, and then spat out. At each step, notes are taken to record the fleeting impressions left by the coffee. Depending upon the system, a rating is applied to the sample. "For maximum accuracy," adds Correa in her article on Colombian *catadores*, "they rate the same coffee again four hours later."

For the discerning layperson, notes jotted in a tasting diary during the cuptasting process can become an ever-evolving record of one's likes and dislikes within the realm of fine coffee.

## Coffee Grower's Terminology

GROWERS AND SELLERS OF COFFEE have developed a terminology in general use for specific coffee-crop qualities or out-of-the-ordinary beans:

*Aged.* Some green coffees may occasionally be stored in a warehouse for as long as several years—this diminishes their acidity and increases their body.

*Green Coffee.* Processed, unroasted coffee beans.

*Hard Bean.* A term for Latin American coffees that, grown at high altitudes, produce particularly dense beans.

*High Grown.* Coffees grown at an altitude above 2,000 feet (625m), generally superior to those grown at lower levels.

*Maragogipe.* The term for a Brazilian variety of *arabica* that thrives at low altitudes in tropical heat, and has now been cultivated in such areas worldwide. Produces very large, attractive beans that nevertheless will generally display the cup characteristics of wherever they were grown.

*Natural.* Another term for coffee processed by the ancient "dry" method.

*Peaberry.* A fairly common coffee mutation that causes a single, rounded, pealike bean (instead of two beans) to form at the center of the coffee berry. Though the beans are attractive, and often separated out for special sale, the mutation has no real effect on aroma, flavor, or body.

*Washed.* Refers to coffee beans processed by the "wet" method.

# Coffee-Taster's Terminology

Those who buy, sell, and evaluate coffee for a living have evolved a complex terminology every bit as exacting as that used for assessing and appreciating fine wines.

While the average coffee drinker may, at first glance, simply take the straightforward, sensible, "I-know-what-I-like" approach to the drink, a brief scan of the terms that follow may offer insight as to why a particular variety or blend of coffee pleases one palate more than another. Learning to isolate those characteristics that make a cup of coffee right for you can in turn lead you toward new, even more pleasurable, coffee choices. And isn't pleasure, after all, the main reason most of us drink coffee in the first place?

The following terms are among those used most frequently by coffee professionals.

**Acidy.** Pleasantly sharp-tasting. The more "acid" coffee tastes, the more bite it has in the mouth. There is no direct correspondence between this quality, however, and the presence of any true acidic elements as measured by pH.

**Aftertaste.** The taste and Bouquet left in the mouth after coffee is swallowed.

**Aged.** Beans stored for a year or more prior to roasting—a wait that reduces acid while developing Sweetness and Body.

**Aroma.** The scent emanating from hot, just-brewed coffee.

**Baked.** Possessing an underdeveloped flavor, the result of insufficient roasting at low temperatures.

**Bitter.** An undesirable flavor component detected at the back of the tongue, usually the result of overroasting.

**Bland.** Soft or Neutral in taste.

**Body.** How a coffee is physically perceived in the mouth, described favorably with such terms as full, heavy, or thick, unfavorably as Thin or slight; good body usually goes hand in hand with rich Flavor and Aroma.

**Bouquet.** The complex combination of a coffee's Aroma, Fragrance, and Aftertaste.

**Bright.** A term sometimes used for coffee with good, pleasant acidity.

**Burnt.** A bitter, acrid flavor sometimes found in overly dark-roasted coffees.

**Buttery.** A coffee whose full flavor and oily Mouthfeel bring to mind the richness of butter.

**Caramelly.** Reminiscent in taste of a cooked sugar syrup, resulting from a change in the coffee beans' carbohydrate content during roasting.

**Carbony.** Tasting Burnt, as in some dark-roasted coffees.

**Chocolatey.** Bringing to mind the richness and sweetness of high-quality chocolate.

**Cinnamony.** A light, sweet, spicy flavor reminiscent of cinnamon.

**Clean.** Coffee whose flavors are clear and untainted.

**Cocoay.** A thin taste of cocoa, usually associated with Stale coffee.

**Dead.** Like Flat, lacking in distinctive Aroma, Fragrance, or Aftertaste; sometimes particularly used to denote a coffee lacking in acidity.

**Delicate.** A subtle aspect of Flavor detected by the tip of the tongue.

**Dirty.** Tasting unclean in some way.

**Earthy.** Like Dirty, tasting of the earth.

**Flat.** Lacking a distinctive Fragrance, Aroma, or Aftertaste.

**Flavor.** The taste sensation of the coffee once it has been swirled around the mouth, described in terms of Acidity, Aroma, and Body, along with more specific comparisons to the flavors of other foods.

**Floral.** Having a subtle Fragrance pleasantly reminiscent of flowers, present in lighter roasts more often than in darker.

**Fragrance.** Related to a coffee's Aroma, discerned by sniffing the brew—described in various terms ranging from Floral to Fruity, Nutty to Spicy.

**Fruity.** A coffee whose Aroma or Taste is reminiscent of fruit, particularly citrus or berries; may be used in a positive or, less often, a negative sense.

**Grassy.** Possessing an unpleasantly Green, astringent Aroma and Taste that brings to mind a just-mown lawn.

**Green.** Coffee that tastes sharp and herbaceous, usually resulting from too-early harvesting or underroasting.

**Groundy.** Tasting Musty or Earthy, usually due to improper storage.

**Hard.** A coffee that is neither Mild nor Sweet; sometimes used for coffees that smell of iodine.

**Harsh.** Unpleasantly Hard or crude in Flavor and Mouthfeel, related to Rioy, and usually resulting from coffee berries allowed to dry on the tree.

**Hidy.** Tasting of leather, usually due to the beans' close contact with animal hides during storage or shipping.

**Lifeless.** Lacking in acidity due to underbrewing. See Thin.

**Light.** An adjective used to modify descriptions of acidity, Aroma, or Body.

**Mellow.** Smooth and well-rounded in flavor, without much (if any) acidity.

**Mild.** Lacking in any distinctive character.

**Mouthfeel.** How the brewed coffee liquid actually feels on contact with the tongue and palate.

**Muddy.** A dullness of Flavor resulting from agitated or unsettled grounds.

**Musty.** An Aroma or Flavor reminiscent of mildew, resulting sometimes by accident—in coffees poorly dried or improperly stored—and sometimes, in the case of certain coffees, by design.

**Neutral.** Lacking in any Strong characteristics—a desirable trait in coffees used as the base for blends.

**Nutty.** Having an Aroma or taste reminiscent of roasted nuts—a positive characteristic if the coffee has good, distinctive Aroma, Flavor, and Body, a negative one if the latter qualities are lacking.

**Papery.** Sometimes applied to light-roasted coffees that lack darker brews' characteristic toasted Flavor.

**Past-Croppish.** Coffee that tastes Strawy or Woody, usually resulting from green beans stored past their prime.

**Quaker.** A bad bean that can spoil a batch of coffee.

**Rancid.** A very Sour or unpleasant Flavor.

**Rich.** A coffee with intense, full Aroma, Flavor, or Aftertaste.

**Rioy.** Having a noticeable, unpleasant medicinal Flavor, often associated with coffees from Brazil's Rio growing district; or having a grainy, starchy Flavor and Mouthfeel.

**Rough.** Producing a parched feeling on the tongue, like sharp or salty flavors.

**Rubbery.** Exhibiting the Aroma and taste of burnt rubber, most often the result of coffee berries allowed to dry before picking, and often found in *robusta* beans.

**Soft.** A coffee that does not affect the tongue in any discernible way, unlike Rough, Rubbery, or Tannic samples; often applied to coffees lacking acidity.

**Sour.** A coffee that tastes excessively sour, usually due to underripe beans; not related to acidity.

**Spicy.** Attractive liveliness of Aroma or Flavor reminiscent of sweet or savory spices.

**Stale.** Used to describe the Aroma and Flavor of coffee brewed from roasted beans that have been stored too long.

**Stinker.** A bad bean that can affect the taste of a batch of roasted coffee.

**Strawy.** Tasting of hay or straw, usually resulting from green beans that have been stored so long that they are past their prime.

**Strong.** An adjective usually applied to Flavor descriptions to indicate their intensity.

**Sweet.** Smooth, palatable, and free from Taints.

**Taint.** An unexpected Flavor resulting from chemical changes produced at any stage during growing, processing, or roasting.

**Tannic.** Displaying the astringent characteristics of tannic acid, resulting in a puckery, biting sensation on the tongue like that caused by some red wines or strong teas.

**Thin.** Lacking in Flavor, Body, or acidity, sometimes inherent in the beans themselves and sometimes due to underbrewing.

**Toasty.** Possessing a pleasant Flavor and Aroma akin to toast, present in well-roasted coffees.

**Turpeny.** A taste reminiscent of turpentine.

**Vinegary.** Having a sharp, sweetish Flavor like vinegar.

**Watery.** A coffee brewed with too much water, resulting in insufficient Flavor and Body.

**Wild.** Used to describe a coffee that has distinctively unusual characteristics of Aroma or Flavor, whether pleasant or unpleasant; or more specifically, a coffee that tastes gamey or spoiled.

**Winey.** Full-bodied and smooth with anywhere from a hint to a distinctive note of acid, like a fine red wine.

**Woody.** Tasting and smelling of wood, usually from extended storage in wooden sheds.

*The coffee pot as art: Yet Another Distorted World View #1, by George Bowes, 1989.*

# Roasting Coffee

We owe a debt of gratitude to the unknown person who, centuries ago, first discovered the magical transformation that occurs when coffee beans are subjected to intense, dry heat.

At a temperature ranging from 400 to 500 degrees Fahrenheit (205–260°C), the beans gradually lose any residual moisture, expanding with a loud "pop" reminiscent of the sound of popping corn. They then begin to darken. The beans' interior cellular structures break down, releasing volatile aromatic oils and other flavor agents, which gradually develop as the beans grow darker, but ultimately deteriorate as they get very dark in color. Meanwhile, complex polysaccharides present in the green beans are transformed by heat into starches and then into sugars, which caramelize, contributing to the coffee's color and flavor.

Different varieties of coffee beans will not only roast differently—developing different characteristics at different heats or stages of the process—but also best present their own complex profiles of characteristics at different levels of roastings. So the art of roasting requires knowledge—both of coffee beans and of the process itself—along with experience and a keen nose and eyes.

There are several stages or degrees to which coffee beans are commonly roasted for brewing, described below from lightest to darkest. Many possess more than one designation, and there is some overlap between categories

*A coffee plantation thrives in the rainforest region of Costa Rica.*

that can sometimes lead to a lack of consistency between what one dealer and the next may refer to as a specific degree of roasting.

***Cinnamon Roast*** is the usual designation for the lightest roast of coffee, in which the beans reach a light brown shade resembling the sweet spice. Many commercial brands of ground coffee get this generally ineffectual treatment, which accounts for their characteristically sour, green taste and lack of body. Also known as Institutional, New England, Half City, or just Light Roast.

***American Roast*** beans have a light-to-medium color and a matte, dry surface. Their flavor is still acidy, but has also developed some balancing sweetness and richness. May also be called Medium Roast.

***City Roast,*** a slight shade darker than American, will usually have lost its acidy tang.

***Full City Roast*** beans are a rich, deep brown in color, and have a more fully developed, richer coffee flavor. Also known sometimes as High Roast or, when spots of oil just begin to emerge on the surface, Light French.

***Continental Roast*** coffee yields beans in which further exposure to heat begins to bring oils to their surfaces, resulting in a glossy sheen. They begin to acquire just a hint of the sweet, smoky taste associated with darker roasts. May also be called Dark Roast, as well as French or Italian Roast, though these latter often apply to still darker shades.

***Espresso Roast*** beans are generally the darkest of all (though some specialty dealers sell "espresso" beans or blends roasted lighter than dark roasts they refer to as Continental, Italian, or French). Almost black and very oily, the beans have a pleasantly burnt flavor that takes precedence over characteristic coffee tastes and smells.

*A neon sign in the window of a coffee store in America's Pacific Northwest jauntily declares the availability of just-roasted beans.*

## Buying & Storing Coffee

We live in a fortunate age that has seen specialty coffee businesses grow and spread like never before. From large cities to small towns, shops selling a wide selection of freshly roasted coffee varieties and blends make it ever easier for people who love good coffee to buy and brew beans that precisely suit their tastes.

But you shouldn't blindly accept coffee merchants' wares just because they use the word "gourmet" or display bin after bin of attractive beans. Look for someone who clearly respects and cares for not only the product but the customer as well.

Remember, first, that the very fact that roasting develops a coffee bean's wonderfully aromatic flavor means that the flavor—once the bean has been roasted— will quickly dissipate. So seek out shops that roast their own beans on-site, or that have a large enough turnover to ensure that you won't be getting stale beans several weeks old. Be wary of loose beans on display in shops such as supermarkets and delicatessens that don't necessarily have a quick turnover of specialty beans; ask direct questions if you have any doubts. And note that some mail-order coffee specialists take pride that the beans they ship their customers by overnight or second-day delivery have been roasted more recently than those purchased in some stores.

Remember that roasted coffee has two natural enemies: heat and air. The first causes the coffee's volatile flavor oils

*An old-fashioned, hand-cranked grinder reliably, if somewhat slowly, provides ready-to-brew coffee.*

to dissipate; the second, in effect, whisks them away. But there are several strategies for combatting these enemies. Buy your coffee as whole beans; grinding exposes more of those oils to the air, making bulk-ground coffee stale in just a day or two. And buy it in relatively small quantities— no more than you would use in a week or so—so that you'll always have beans that have been roasted fairly recently.

At home, store your coffee beans in an airtight jar and keep them somewhere cool—the refrigerator or, if there's room, the freezer. You'll be amazed at how such simple strategies preserve the full flavor of freshly roasted coffee.

# A Guide to Coffee Selection

Use the following descriptions as your guide to selecting coffees that suit your own particular taste; choose several different varieties or blends, if you wish, to have on hand for different moods or occasions, or to offer guests individually brewed cups to their liking.

And bear in mind that coffee has such a complex taste that no two people's opinions of what makes a good cup are likely to be identical. Identify those characteristics that please you most, and look for them most specifically in the coffees you select.

## Unblended Coffees

**African**

Generally considered to be well-rounded coffees with medium to full body and a notable acidity; often characterized as having floral or winey qualities.

***Angola.*** Produces mostly *robusta*, though some *arabica* beans—somewhat flat in character, but good for blending—are also grown.

***Bugisu.*** See *Uganda.*

***Bukoba.*** See *Tanzania.*

***Burundi.*** Produces full-bodied, acidy *arabica* beans of very good to excellent quality.

***Cameroon.*** That half of the West African nation's crop composed of *arabica* beans is mellow and sweet, of very good to excellent quality.

***Chagga.*** See *Kenya.*

***Djimmah.*** See *Ethiopia.*

***Ethiopia.*** Beans from the *Djimmah* region, where *arabica* coffee reputedly originated, are earthy and spicy, with big body and a somewhat pungent aftertaste. *Harrar,* also known as Ethiopian *Mocca,* produces an intense, winelike coffee popular as the dominant element in blends.

***Harrar.*** See *Ethiopia.*

***Ituri.*** See *Zaire.*

***Kenya.*** Full-bodied, smooth, with a generous touch of acidity and flavor and fragrance comparable to a fine wine, Kenya's *arabica* coffees have an outstanding reputation. Top-grade Kenya beans are designated "AA." Excellent Kenyan coffee also comes from the *Chagga* tribe, who grow it on the slopes of Mt. Kilimanjaro.

***Kilimanjaro.*** See *Kenya* and *Tanzania.*

**Kivu.** See *Zaire.*

**Mocca.** See *Ethiopia.*

**Mocha.** See *Yemen.*

**Rwanda.** Very high-quality *arabica* beans from this nation yield a rich, very acidy, dark-colored cup of coffee.

**Tanzania.** As good as those of *Kenya, arabicas* from *Tanzania* present a complex composition of body, acidy and winelike qualities, and mellow flavor. Of particular note are those from *Kilimanjaro* and Plantation *Bukoba.*

**Uganda.** A rarity among this country's so-so *robustas* is the very good *arabica* coffee known as *Bugisu.*

**Yemen.** Noted for the exceptional *arabica* coffee named after the now-closed port of *Mocha* whose full-bodied, bittersweet personality recalls in some people's minds the taste of fine chocolate, even though a cup of true *Mocha* coffee contains not a trace of the cacao bean.

**Zaire.** Produces mostly *robusta* beans, with the outstanding exception of the full-bodied, distinctively acidy *arabica* beans from the *Kivu* and *Ituri* districts.

**Zimbabwe.** A less acidy but fuller-bodied *arabica* coffee than those of *Kenya.*

### American & Caribbean
Generally characterized as well-balanced, with medium body, good acidity, and a floral quality.

**Amatitlan.** See *Guatemala.*

**Antigua.** See *Guatemala.*

**Armenia.** See *Colombia.*

**Barahona.** See *Dominican Republic.*

**Blue Mountain.** See *Jamaica.*

**Bourbon Santos.** See *Brazil.*

**Brazil.** The world's largest producer of coffee beans, mostly *arabica* of little distinctive character but excellent for blending. One notable exception is Brazilian *Bourbon Santos,* a very good, smooth, and mild variety.

**Colombia.** The world's second-largest producer of coffee beans, and the leader in fine *arabica* coffees. Of note are those from Medellin, whose richness and full body are offset by a touch of acidity; *Armenia,* somewhat thinner and less acidy, but still exhibiting good aroma, body, and flavor characterized by a winey touch; and rich, acidy, somewhat less subtle Manizales. Also keep an eye out for what is known as Vintage Colombian: coffee aged in its green state for up to eight years, which develops a sweet, syrupy richness free of acidity. The two highest grades of Colombian beans are Supremo (the best) and Excelso.

**Costa Rica.** Central America's strongest coffees, marked by sharp acidity and heavy flavor and body.

**Cuba.** Produces a smallish crop of *arabica* beans used most often in blending for their heavy, somewhat flat flavor.

**Cucutas.** See *Venezuela.*

**Dominican Republic.** A rich, moderately acidy coffee. Those from *Barahona* are particularly full-bodied; beans from *Santo Domingo* are marked by a pleasant sweetness.

**El Salvador.** The best are High Grown beans that, though somewhat lacking in aroma, are noted for their mild, slightly sweet flavor, good body, and moderate acidity.

**Guatemala.** High-mountain coffees from *Amatitlan*, *Antigua*, and Coban have high acidity, heavy body, and a pleasing hint of smokiness or spice.

**Haiti.** The best are richly flavored beans with a hint of sweetness, heavy body, and medium acidity, particularly good when dark roasted.

**Hawaii.** Almost always known as *Kona* coffee, after the prime growing district on the slopes of the Mauna Loa volcano. Characterized by abundant body, aroma, richness, spiciness, and sweetness that rank it among the world's greatest coffees.

**Honduras.** A pleasant if indistinct coffee with mild flavor, medium acidity, and light body.

**Jamaica.** Most Jamaican coffees are noteworthy for their fine, mellow flavor. Most legendary is *Blue Mountain* coffee, grown high atop that landmark and prized worldwide for its full body, light acidity, and wonderfully mellow aroma and flavor. But more coffee winds up sold worldwide as Blue Mountain than is actually produced there; buy only from the most reputable dealers.

**Kona.** See *Hawaii*.

**Merida.** See *Venezuela*.

**Mexico.** The best of Mexico's coffees are characterized by their excellent fragrance, rich flavor, full body, and mild acidity.

**Nicaragua.** Seek out high-quality, high-grown varieties, which have a mild flavor and moderate acidity.

**Panama.** Production is limited, but the best beans show mild flavor accompanied by distinctive body and acidity.

**Peru.** Though lacking somewhat in body, the best of Peru's coffees have good flavor with just a trace of acidity.

**Santo Domingo.** See *Dominican Republic.*

**Tachiras.** See *Venezuela.*

**Venezuela.** Beans from *Cucutas* and *Tachiras* have much in common with rich, somewhat acidy *Colombian* beans. *Merida* coffee has less acidity but very good flavor and delicate body.

## Indonesian & Asian

For the most part full-bodied coffees lacking in acidity but possessing earthiness and unusual, beguiling aromas and flavors.

**Celebes.** *Kalosi* beans from this Indonesian island are sharply acidy and have so much body they seem almost syrupy.

**China.** Grown in the *Yunnan* Province, China's coffees are rich, full-bodied, slightly acidy, and contain a trace of sweetness.

**India.** Those named after the region once known as *Mysore* produce a dark brew with full body and slight acidity. More rich, yet delicate, is Indian *Malabar.*

**Java.** Though a lot of coffee now coming from the island is *robusta* and *liberica*, good-quality Java *arabicas* are noted for spicy aroma, heavy body, and low acidity.

**Kalosi.** See *Celebes.*

**Malabar.** See *India.*

**Mandheling.** See *Sumatra.*

*Mysore.* See *India.*

*New Guinea.* Richly flavored *arabica* coffees with light body and aroma.

*Sumatra.* Scarce but good-quality *arabica* beans that make a rich, mellow, full-bodied cup with low acidity. Best of all is *Mandheling,* characterized by a heavy, syrupy taste and body.

*Timor.* Comparable to the best of *Sumatra* and *Java,* Timor's coffees have good aroma and flavor, heavy body, and mild acidity.

*Yunnan.* See *China.*

## Blended Coffees

Two or more different varieties of coffee are frequently blended together in varying proportions to produce a brew with its own distinctive characteristics of aroma, flavor, and body. While the possibilities are endless and names often up to the whim of the merchant, here are some of the most common combinations.

*Breakfast.* A well-balanced blend usually made up of smooth, mild Brazilian Santos and more acidic and wine-like African beans, in equal proportion. Sometimes, Colombian coffee is also added for its body and flavor.

*House Blend.* A catchall term for whatever and however many different kinds of beans the store owner fancies make a well-balanced cup. Ask before sampling.

*Mocha-Java.* A balancing of Mocha's winey, acidy characteristics with the lush body and sweetness of a Java. While many blends may call themselves this, true Mocha-Java is rare; usually, beans from neighboring countries that exhibit similar characteristics are used.

*Neapolitan.* A favorite dark, heavy, Italian-style roast featuring Brazilian Santos and a rich African *arabica* coffee.

*New Orleans.* A blend in which acidy Brazilian beans are combined in a three- or four-to-one ratio with chicory—a root whose flavor, when roasted, vaguely approximates that of coffee—to produce a sharp, pungent brew favored in that city.

*Roma.* A combination of a dark-roasted, New Orleans blend with an even darker, espresso-roasted, Italian coffee.

*Viennese.* A popular Austrian-style blend usually consisting of two parts high-quality Mexican beans, roasted to a Full City roast, and one part good Venezuelan coffee, roasted to a dark, French roast.

## Flavored Coffees

These demand to be mentioned if for no other reason than that they are responsible for such a significant part of the growth of specialty coffee sales in recent years. Roasted coffee beans are spray-coated with flavoring agents that, after grinding, impart their own complementary (that is, if you like them) and virtually calorie-free dessert-like flavor to that of the coffee itself. Some popular flavors from the seemingly ever-burgeoning list of choices:

| | |
|---|---|
| Almond | Cinnamon |
| Amaretto | Frangelico |
| Chocolate | Hazelnut |

| Irish Cream | Mint |
| Kahlua | Orange |
| Macadamia Nut | Raspberry |
| Mandarin Orange | Vanilla |

## Decaffeinated Coffee

The majority of coffee drinkers value the beverage for the eye-opening stimulation it gives them—a result of the caffeine present in the beans. Medical opinion continues to be divided on whether or not caffeine is potentially harmful or relatively harmless; to be sure, in the relatively small quantities of the drink most people consume, caffeine is generally viewed as more of a good than a bad thing.

Yet, a significant number of coffee drinkers love the flavor but would prefer to do without the caffeine—for reasons relating to their health, or because they'd like a cup of coffee in the evening without the threat of insomnia. To that end, two basic processes have been developed to remove most of the caffeine present in coffee beans.

The challenge in both methods is to eliminate caffeine—in itself a flavorless substance—without diminishing the coffee's flavor. The most effective way of achieving this is through the use of the solvent methylene chloride. Green coffee beans are soaked in a bath of very warm water, which plumps them up and brings the caffeine to their surfaces. The solvent is then applied—removing the caffeine without harming the coffee's volatile oils—and rinsed away, generally taking with it 97 to 99 percent of the caffeine. Any traces of the solvent, which evaporates at 114 degrees Fahrenheit (45°C), vanish when the beans are roasted at temperatures exceeding 400 degrees Fahrenheit (205°C).

Still, those who care about caffeine as a health issue may also be concerned that a chemical solvent has been applied to their decaf beans, even if laboratory tests cannot detect a trace of it in the roasted coffee. If that is a concern of yours, seek out coffee decaffeinated by the Swiss water process, which removes the substance with hot water, steam, and charcoal filtration. But be advised that, unlike the use of a caffeine-selective solvent, this process also tends to remove some of the coffee's volatile oils. The resulting coffee may lack somewhat in flavor.

Whichever kind of decaf you choose, seek out freshly roasted whole beans and store and prepare them as you would any other fine coffee.

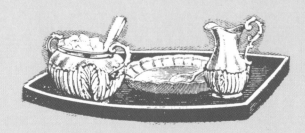

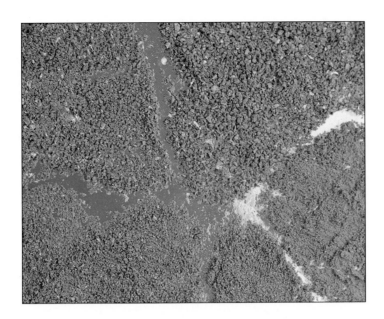

# Grinding Coffee

Unground, coffee's flavor remains locked up in the bean. Grinding creates myriad tiny surfaces from which hot water can extract the roasted coffee's flavor elements in the brewing process.

Two types of machines are available to do this essential job in the home; though the term "grinder" is generally applied to both, only one truly merits the name. That is the electric or hand-cranked coffee mill or burr-type grinder, which actually crushes the beans between rough metal plates. This adjustable machine, fairly high in price compared to the other option, yields uniform particles of coffee to suit whichever brewing method is used.

More common nowadays are electric grinders equipped with a chamber housing a small, propellerlike double blade that chops up the beans at superfast speed. Though convenient and relatively inexpensive, these machines do not yield a uniform grind, though uniformity can be increased by gently shaking the grinder during use. Furthermore, while the burr-type grinder controls the fineness or coarseness of the coffee by how close or far apart its burrs are set, fineness with a blade grinder is more arbitrary: it is all too easy for the inexperienced user to produce a grind that is not quite suited to his or her brewing equipment. You might want to ask your coffee dealer to provide you with a tiny sample of beans correctly ground for your purposes, to use as a point of reference; or refer to the photographs shown here.

The degree of grind you choose is solely a matter of how you will brew the coffee. The basic rule is the less time the ground coffee will be in contact with the water, the finer the grind must be for all its flavor to be extracted. Here are the four basic grinds, along with the brewing methods to which they apply.

*Coarse Grind.* For percolators, or for making cold-water coffee concentrate. Generally achieved in five to seven seconds in a blade-type grinder.

*Medium Grind.* For jugs, plunger pots, or drip coffee makers using flat-bottomed filters. Equivalent to about ten seconds with a blade-type grinder.

*Fine Grind.* For vacuum pots, Neapolitan pots, Turkish coffee, and cone-shaped drip filters. Achieved in fifteen to twenty seconds with a blade grinder.

*Extra-Fine Grind.* For use in espresso machines. Achieved in twenty-five to thirty seconds with a blade grinder.

*From the coarsest textures for percolation to the finest for espresso, roasted coffee may be freshly ground to suit any brewing method (previous page).*

*A lineup of coffee-brewing equipment (right). Clockwise from left: percolator, Italian stovetop espresso pot, three home countertop espresso machines, electric drip machine, standard drip filter and pot, plunger pot, electric grinders, and Middle Eastern ibrik.*

# Brewing Methods

Every coffee lover has—or yearns to have—his or her own beloved, ideal way of brewing coffee. If you've already found yours, perhaps the following guidelines will lead you to a new discovery, or help you reach new tastes with your tried-and-true method. If you're still searching, let this survey be your guide.

**Ibrik.** The small, long-handled pot used for brewing Middle Eastern-style Turkish or Greek coffee. See page 65 for basic instructions.

**Jug.** An old-fashioned method in which hot water is poured over medium-grind coffee in an earthenware jug and left to steep for four to five minutes, then carefully poured to avoid grounds in the cup.

**Plunger pot.** A modern variation on the jug method, much favored by coffee lovers. The jug is replaced by a straight-sided glass or pottery cylinder topped by a lid through which passes a plunger rod attached to a fine metal filter that fits snugly inside the cylinder. Once the coffee has steeped, the plunger is pressed down, forcing all the grounds to the bottom of the pot.

**Drip filter.** Many variations of this exist: electric automatic makers with cone-shaped or flat-bottomed filters; pour-it-yourself filters and carafes of varying sizes; even the two-chambered Neapolitan pot, which is assembled with ground coffee sandwiched between its two halves, brought to a boil, then inverted so the hot water drips down through the coffee into the serving pot. Produces good, reliable coffee, if just a touch bland to some tastes. Some with sensitive palates claim they can taste the filter paper in the brew, and may opt for one of the gold-plated (though not *too* expensive), permanent, washable filters now available.

**Vacuum.** An elegant technique invented in 1840 by Scottish engineer Robert Napier, now outmoded due to the fragility of its equipment, it still has some devotees for the fine-tasting coffee it produces. Water is brought to a boil in the lower of the device's two glass globes; steam forces it up through a glass tube into the upper chamber, which contains ground coffee. After a few minutes of steeping, the pot is removed from the heat; the change of temperature forms a vacuum in the lower chamber, causing the coffee to filter through a screen back into the lower chamber, which detaches for pouring.

**Percolation.** Percolation is so much a part of the twentieth-century coffee lover's consciousness that its devotees will swear it makes good coffee—despite the fact that the method is likely to result in a boiled-tasting brew. As water comes to a boil in the percolator, it is forced up a metal stem into a filter basket containing coarsely ground coffee, through which it drips back into the bottom of the pot, recirculating until the desired strength is reached. Electric percolators regulate brewing temperatures more carefully, shutting off when the coffee is ready to drink.

*Espresso machine.* A fundamental piece of equipment not just in Italian establishments but wherever good coffee is enjoyed worldwide—even in the home today, thanks to small countertop models now available. For instructions and espresso terminology, see page 75.

*Dutch coffee concentrate.* A little-known method perfected in the nineteenth century by Dutch settlers in Java. For instructions, see page 91.

*A long-handled, narrow-necked* ibrik *is the device of choice for brewing traditional Turkish or Greek coffee (opposite page).*

*On a Costa Rican plantation in the Heredia province, workers kneel in the fields to handsort just-picked coffee beans (left).*

*Having been piled up and covered overnight, coffee beans are raked out to dry in the morning sun on a Colombian plantation.*

## Basic Guidelines for Brewing Perfect Coffee

WHATEVER BREWING METHOD YOU OPT FOR, A FEW basic principles apply that will ensure optimal results:

*Use fresh, cold water.* Remember that a cup of coffee contains more water than it does coffee! That water's quality will be reflected in the final cup. If your area has good, drinkable tap water, use it, letting the tap run a few seconds before filling the kettle or coffee maker. If you wouldn't dream of drinking water from your tap, don't subject your coffee to it: brew with filtered or bottled water.

*Use good-quality, freshly roasted coffee beans.* See the preceding pages for a guide to selecting the right coffee for you.

*Grind the coffee properly, just before brewing.* See the preceding guidelines on grinding. Never brew a second batch with already-used grounds!

*Use the right amount of coffee.* In general, brew with two tablespoons (30ml) of ground coffee for every six ounces (19ml) of water (one "cup" of coffee). Adjust these proportions to taste, if necessary.

*Use clean equipment.* Wash your brewing equipment after each use with warm, soapy water, then rinse well. The volatile oils in coffee can coat utensils and eventually turn rancid, giving your coffee an unpleasant flavor.

*Don't use boiling water.* Water at the boiling point will harm or dissipate some of the volatile oils in coffee, preventing their flavors from ever reaching you. Once your kettle boils, remove from the heat and let it rest a minute before pouring into drip filters; *regulate heat carefully when using other coffee makers.* (Automatic makers should have built-in thermostats that regulate water temperature.)

*Beware of reheating coffee.* If you must reheat coffee, warm very, very gently over the lowest heat possible, lest it boil and develop an unpleasant "stewed" flavor. Coffee can be kept warm on a hot plate or other warmer—including those built into some electric makers—for no more than about twenty minutes before its flavor turns. Instead, try transferring just-brewed coffee to one of the modern vacuum-insulated pots expressly designed to keep it drinkable for hours.

# Coffee & Liqueurs

Coffee has always been such a natural after-dinner beverage that it makes perfect sense to pair it with a complementary after-dinner drink—or even to imbue a liqueur with coffee's own rich savor. Of the former, the options are virtually unlimited, and this brief list offers a few favorites that begin to suggest the broad range of choices. And the ranks of liqueurs that take their flavor from coffee continue to grow.

**After-Dinner Companions to Coffee**
Try sipping a small glass of one of these spirits or liqueurs along with your coffee; or, if you like, pour directly into your coffee cup!

*Amaretto.* An Italian liqueur that marries almond and apricot; good alongside or in the coffee cup.

*Bailey's Irish Cream.* The one that initiated the craze for cream-based liqueurs. For those who like this sort of thing, this mild, whiskey-flavored concoction is delightful accompanying or combined with coffee.

*Benedictine.* A sweet, herbal French elixir that, when poured into the hot brew, produces a drink sometimes known as Monk's Coffee.

*Brandy.* As well as rich, savory grape brandy, sample the wide variety of brandies distilled from other fruits, each of which carries its own distinctive natural essence.

*Cheri-Suisse.* Swiss cherry-chocolate liqueur.

*Cognac.* The greatest of grape brandies—and an elegant companion to fine coffee. Poured into the coffee, cognac makes a drink sometimes called Royal Coffee.

*Crème de Noix.* French hazelnut liqueur from the Perigord region.

*Curaçao.* Orange-flavored liqueurs, most notable of which are Cointreau and Grand Marnier.

*Drambuie.* A sweet liqueur based on Scottish malt whisky. With coffee, Drambuie creates Prince Charles Coffee.

*Peppermint Schnapps.* Intensely minty and dry; a bracing accompaniment.

*Rum.* May be sipped alongside or combined with coffee to make an exotic cup of Caribbean Coffee.

*Sambuca.* A clear, bracing, licorice-flavored Italian liqueur. In one tradition, three roasted coffee beans are floated atop a small glass of the liqueur, whose surface is then set alight, yielding a Sambuca *con Mosca*—"with flies."

*Vandermint.* Dutch chocolate-mint liqueur.

*Whiskey.* The best Irish whiskeys and Scotch single malts are so complex that they merit after-dinner sipping, and complement coffee wonderfully. Pour into the cup for an Irish or Scotch Coffee—whether or not you sweeten the brew and float heavy cream on top to make the popular American bar drink.

## Coffee-Flavored Liqueurs

Though coffee itself predominates in the flavors of these and other after-dinner liqueurs, they nevertheless merit serving alongside a hot cupful—though you may want to drink the latter black and unsweetened for contrast's sake. By all means, pour the liqueur into your coffee cup—and add cream, if the spirit so moves you!

*Arrow Coffee-Flavored Brandy.* A product of the United States, rich-tasting, yet mild and smooth.

*Bahia.* From Brazil, a bittersweet blend of local coffee and grain spirit.

*Cafe Benedictine.* A blend of coffee and the legendary French herbal liqueur.

*Cafe de Gaetano.* Smooth and syrupy.

*Cafe di Torani.* Coffee flavors heavily tinged with caramel and chocolate; made in the United States.

*Caffe Lolita.* From Mexico, a good flavor of well-roasted coffee in a thick, sweet base.

*Caffeto.* A Colombian liqueur distinguished by the strong flavor and color of good espresso.

*Coffee House.* A rich, robust blend from the Virgin Islands.

*Crème de Cafe—"Coffee Sport."* A light, lively U.S. liqueur.

*DeKuyper Coffee Liqueur.* A sweet and syrupy U.S. liqueur.

*Dos Santos.* Mild, sweet, and smooth; from Mexico.

*Expresso.* An Italian, espresso-flavored liqueur.

*Gallweys Irish Coffee.* A dark, rich, and smooth blend of coffee, Irish whiskey, honey, and herbs.

*Hiram Walker Coffee-Flavored Brandy.* From the United States, a combination of well-roasted coffee flavor, brandy, and just a suspicion of chocolate.

*Kahlua.* One of the greats; a Mexican, candy-sweet blend of good coffee flavor with a touch of vanilla.

*Kamora.* Also from Mexico; dark in color, with a suggestion of caramel.

*Keoki.* A Hawaiian specialty flavored with Kona coffee.

*Kozana.* Mild, sweet, and smooth; from Mexico.

*Kukul.* A Mexican blend of coffee and chocolate flavors.

*Mokka Mit Sahne.* A German coffee-cream liqueur.

*Mount Kenya.* Has the excellent flavor of Kenyan coffee.

*Old Jamaica Blue Mountain.* A strong-flavored blend of Jamaica's most famous coffee and island rum.

*Old Vienna.* A Viennese blend of coffee and cognac.

*Royal French Coffee-Chocolate.* A French liqueur blending good-quality coffee and chocolate flavors with milk.

*Sabra Coffee Liqueur.* A complex-flavored Israeli liqueur with fine aroma, taste, and texture.

*Serrana.* A syrupy Mexican liqueur with a hint of smoke to its coffee flavor.

*Tia Maria.* Jamaica's famous liqueur features well-roasted Blue Mountain coffee flavors with local rum and spices.

3

# OLD WORLD TRADITIONS

$T$he bags are packed and the visas have been gathered for an evocative eating and drinking tour of the lands where coffee first rose to public acclaim. As the nine following descriptions vividly demonstrate, each country where coffee is consumed has wholeheartedly adopted the beverage as its own and adapted it to local customs. This means that, with a little planning and preparation—and a drop of imagination— a pot of coffee and a few simple accompaniments are sufficient to carry you thousands of miles away, within the comfort of your own home.

*Lifelong habitués of a Salzburg, Austria, coffeehouse while away the morning discussing the day's news, smoking cigarettes, and sipping cups of heady brew (page 62).*

*An assortment of Turkish serving dishes on display at a grand bazaar in Turkey (right).*

# Turkish After-Dinner Coffee

In homes and restaurants throughout Turkey, coffee is the ultimate sign of true hospitality. Indeed, so renowned is the Turks' passion for coffee that their style of brewing it—common throughout the Middle East and eastern Mediterranean—has come to be known almost universally outside the region as Turkish coffee.

Set the dinner table lavishly for a Turkish meal featuring roast or stewed lamb and mountains of fragrant rice pilaf. Lay out a richly embroidered tablecloth—the colorful sort you might find in the bazaar. Set a charger of shining, hand-beaten brass or other dazzling metal at each place, upon which your finest china will be laid.

When the dishes have been cleared, retire to the kitchen to grind and brew a fresh pot of fragrant Turkish coffee. Pour it into individual beaten-brass demitasses—or whatever small, straight-sided cups you have. Pass the brew only after you yourself have tasted your own cup—a traditional gesture to your guests demonstrating that no harm will come to them from drinking it. Then, in order of descending rank or prestige, distribute the cups, offering your guests a tray of traditional Turkish sweetmeats to nibble between sips of the sweet, strong brew.

Depending upon the lightheartedness of the occasion, when the last sips have been taken, you might wish to offer your guests brief instruction on how to tell their fortunes from the coffee grounds in their cups. For the sake of impartiality—and greater fun—it might be a good idea to have each person present read the grounds of the guest seated to his or her right or left.

You never know what intrigues may thus arise . . . .

# Brewing Turkish Coffee

Turkish coffee is traditionally brewed in a brass pot known as an *ibrik*, circular and straight-sided, slightly narrower at the top than the bottom, with a long handle that once facilitated heating over an open fire.

The ibrik is used to brew a cup of coffee that is thicker and sweeter than most Westerners are accustomed to—the result of finely pulverized coffee beans and sugar simmered together with water. Middle Eastern spices such as cardamom, cloves, or cinnamon are sometimes ground up with the beans for an especially fragrant cup.

A good head of foam or froth is another hallmark of the brew, a feature encouraged by the narrow opening of the pot. "If the froth is absent from the face of the coffee," goes an old Turkish saying, "the host loses face."

For each guest, you will need:

**1 tablespoon very finely ground Mocha coffee**
**1 small cardamom pod, or 2 cloves, or ½-inch**
  **cinnamon stick, very finely ground (optional)**
**1 demitasse (about 3 ounces) cold water**
**1 teaspoon sugar**

Put coffee, spice, and water into ibrik; depending on size of ibrik and number of guests being served, prepare coffee in batches. Place pot over low to moderate heat and add sugar when coffee boils and froths up. Remove from heat and stir until froth dies down. Return pot to heat until froth rises again; remove and stir.

Return pot one final time to heat; when coffee builds a good head of froth, pour into demitasses, shaking the pot slightly with each pour to transfer some froth to each serving. Serve immediately.

# Telling Fortunes with Turkish Coffee

Many a Middle Eastern coffee drinker still gives some credence to the omens that lurk in the bottom of the cup.

Anyone with a little imagination—and a willing suspension of disbelief—can do likewise. When you've finished the last drop of thick liquid in your cup of Turkish coffee, return the cup to its saucer. With a quick twist of the wrist, invert the cup onto the saucer so the grounds run down the cup's sides.

Wait about five minutes for the grounds to settle into their fate-appointed positions. Then peer into the cup and "read" the patterns. Do rippling waves foretell a vacation at the beach, or the shifting sands of fate? Does a stranger's comely profile appear? Do more abstract patterns somehow relate to an emotion you've been feeling lately?

It is like a three-dimensional Rorschach ink-blot: whatever is seen by you or your fortune-teller has a certain validity. Indeed, Jung might well have seen the cup as yet another conduit into the collective unconscious.

*A plateful of sweet halvah provides a complement to thick, black Turkish coffee.*

### Halvah

This version of the classic Turkish nougat features two different kinds of nuts. Store in an airtight container.

**8 egg whites**
**2 cups granulated sugar**
**¾ cup honey, at room temperature**
**1 cup coarsely chopped roasted almonds**
**1 cup coarsely chopped roasted pistachio nuts**
**1 tablespoon rose water**
**Edible rice paper**

In a round-bottomed mixing bowl, preferably copper, beat egg whites with a wire whisk until they form stiff peaks. Gradually beat in sugar until thoroughly incorporated.

Transfer to top of a double boiler over low heat. Add honey and cook, stirring constantly, until very thick, about 30 minutes. Stir in nuts and rose water.

Line a baking sheet with a layer of rice paper. With a wet spatula, spread mixture about ¾ inch thick on top of paper. Top with another layer of rice paper, place another baking sheet on top, and weight down with kitchen weights or heavy cans. Leave at room temperature for 12 to 24 hours.

Remove weights and, with a large, heavy knife, carefully cut halvah into 1 x 2-inch pieces. Makes about 2 pounds.

*For a Middle Eastern coffee gathering, offer guests a selection of sweet delights such as nut-filled halvah, jellylike loukoumi, roasted nuts, dates, and dried apricots.*

### Loukoumi

This jellylike confection, commonly known in the West as Turkish delight, brings a smile to the lips.

**2 cups granulated sugar**
**1 ¼ cups water**
**1 lemon, juice squeezed, zests cut into thin strips**
**4 tablespoons unflavored gelatin powder**
**3 tablespoons orange-flower water**
**½ cup toasted pine nuts**
**¼ cup powdered sugar**
**2 tablespoons cornstarch**

In a saucepan over moderate heat, stir together granulated sugar and half of the water until sugar dissolves. Add lemon juice, bring to a boil, and simmer 15 minutes.

In a small bowl, soften gelatin in remaining water. Stir into saucepan and boil, stirring occasionally, until mixture reaches about 225 degrees Fahrenheit on a candy thermometer or forms a thin thread when a spoon is lifted from it, about 20 minutes.

Remove from heat and let cool at room temperature about 30 minutes. Then stir in lemon zests, orange-flower water, and pine nuts. Lightly spray an 8 x 8-inch baking pan with flavorless, nonstick spray. Pour mixture into pan and let set at room temperature 24 hours.

In a shallow bowl, stir together powdered sugar and cornstarch. With a knife, cut loukoumi into 1 x 1-inch squares and gently turn them in powdered sugar mixture to coat well. Store in an airtight container, sprinkling more sugar-cornstarch mixture between layers. Makes about 1 pound.

# Greek Afternoon Coffee

On Athens' Omonia Square, afternoon coffee is a daily ritual. Shoppers, business people, and folks on holiday all stop to watch the passing scene in front of legendary Floka's Cafe while they enjoy a steaming little cup of sweet, thick Greek coffee—brewed in the same manner as Turkish coffee—along with a piece of the favorite Middle Eastern honey, nut, and phyllo pastry, *baklava*; an ice cream sundae topped with nuts and drizzled with honey; or perhaps a simple sliced orange, also drizzled with the fragrant and world-renowned Hymettus honey.

Even if you can't locate your own jar of Hymettus' finest, you can certainly recreate any of these Greek specialties with the best local honey available. Baklava, a treat that is somewhat difficult to prepare, can fortunately be found fairly easily in gourmet and Middle Eastern delicatessens and pastry shops.

Set a casual table with a crisp white tablecloth, and stack some sturdy white china dessert plates with pastries and oranges. Chill small glass or metal ice cream dishes in the freezer. Have a large pitcher of ice water at the ready, along with small drinking glasses, to pour the traditional cooling accompaniment to a hot cupful.

To capture a more authentic Greek mood, pop a recording of *bouzouki* music—the kind popularized by the film *Zorba the Greek*—on the stereo; or, for a more romantic note, try an album by Nana Mouskouri or Demis Roussos. If you can find them in an ethnic shop, a few strings of Greek worry beads, plastic or leather loops strung with brightly colored plastic beads, contribute nicely to ambience. In any authentic Greek cafe, you'll see the regulars habitually, absent-mindedly flipping the beads at a rhythmic pace as they read the newspaper or sip their brew.

As for the coffee itself, follow the instructions for Turkish coffee on page 65—only be sure to respectfully call it "Greek coffee" for this occasion. And, in the style of a grand cafe, allow each guest to choose from among the myriad options available for individual cups: boiled once, twice, or three times; using a light, moderate, or heavy amount of ground coffee; and very sweet (*glikos*), moderately sweet (*metrios*), or bitter (*schetos*).

Of course, having given your guests the choice, you can still—as some waiters do—repair to the kitchen and make every cup precisely the same way: medium-bodied, well-boiled, and metrios. Who will know the difference?

---

### *Oranges with Honey*

**6 large, sweet, seedless oranges, chilled in the refrigerator**
**¾ cup honey, at room temperature**
**Fresh mint sprigs**

With a small, sharp knife, carefully remove the orange peels, cutting just deep enough to also remove the pith. Cut the peeled oranges crosswise into ¼- to ½-inch-thick slices and arrange attractively on a serving platter.

Just before serving, drizzle honey evenly over the oranges. Garnish with mint.

*Cool and sweet, a plate of honeyed oranges provides refreshment for Greek-style afternoon coffee.*

### *Honey-Nut Ice Cream Sundaes*

Use the best-quality vanilla ice cream you can find
for these simple, elegant concoctions.

**12 scoops (4 ounces each) vanilla ice cream**
**1 cup honey, at room temperature**
**6 tablespoons coarsely chopped toasted almonds**
**6 tablespoons coarsely chopped toasted walnuts**
**6 tablespoons coarsely chopped toasted pistachio**
  **nuts**

Place 2 scoops ice cream in each of 6 chilled serving
dishes. Drizzle honey generously over ice cream.
Sprinkle with nuts. Serve immediately. Makes 6
servings.

72

*A honey-nut ice cream sundae, accompanied here by wedges of baklava, provides an elegant accompaniment to a cup of Greek coffee.*

# Italian Anytime Coffee with *Biscotti*

Throughout Italy, coffee is enjoyed throughout the day—from the first cup of *caffe latte* sipped in early morning to the last drop of after-dinner espresso.

The options for serving Italian-style coffee in your own home are as widely varied as Italian coffee drinks and as the regional specialties with which they are enjoyed. You can pour a thick, rich brew from a Neapolitan filter pot and pass it around with a tempting ricotta pie or cheese-cake. Or you may opt to serve it with the favorite Milanese fruit bread known as *panettone*—a widely imported specialty available in Italian delicatessens and gourmet markets.

Alternatively, brew up your favorite espresso-based coffee; small countertop machines for the home now make it easy and economical. Pass a selection of simple Italian *biscotti*—bought in the supermarket or at a local specialty bakery, or easily made at home—arranged in a rustic, napkin-lined basket, or on a terra-cotta or white porcelain dish.

For the coffee itself, choose a fairly dark-roasted blend—one labeled "Italian" or "espresso" should do the trick; brew a decaf espresso roast for those guests who have cut down on caffeine. Serve it in heavy, white china demitasses for espresso, and in larger cups of similar weight for cappucino or latte. One good choice is the cup offered by familiar Italian manufacturers of espresso machines or brands of coffee; they have just the right feel, and they also have the added authenticity of being used in many an Italian cafe. If the weather seems too hot for even a die-hard coffee lover to drink the brew hot—it sometimes gets that way during midsummer in Italy—you might instead offer an *espresso granita,* a water ice that offers all of the drink's rich flavor and caffeine boost.

Offer a selection of the latest Italian fashion magazines, picked up at your best local newsstand. And put a favorite opera on the stereo—Puccini, perhaps, or Verdi—to help create the illusion that, just maybe, La Scala Milano lies just outside your window.

## Italian Coffee at Sea

"ANOTHER HEAD—AND A BLACK ALPACA JACKET and a serviette this time—to tell us coffee is ready. Not before it is time, too. We go down into the subterranean state-room and sit on the screw-pin chairs, while the ship does the slide-and-slope trot under us, and we drink a couple of cups of coffee and milk, and eat a piece of bread and butter. At least one of the innumerable members of the crew gives me one cup, then casts me off. It is most obviously his intention that I shall get no more: because of course the innumerable members of the crew could all just do with another coffee and milk. However, though the ship heaves and the alpaca coats cluster menacingly in the doorway, I balance my way to the tin buffet and seize the coffee pot and the milk pot...."

—D.H. Lawrence,
*Sea and Sardinia*

# An Italian Espresso Primer

The exact instructions for making an espresso-based drink will vary somewhat with the home machine you use and its specific mechanism. But the principle remains the same: steam is forced through finely ground, dark-roasted coffee that has been tamped down in a filter insert clamped into the machine. Out emerges a rich, thick coffee essence with an appealing touch of foam on top, known as the *crema*. Serve the coffee with sugar, if you like, but avoid the non-Italian affectation of a strip of lemon peel.

The steam may also be channeled through a spigot that injects it into a pitcher of milk, resulting in the hot and frothy addition that produces cappucino, latte, and other similar drinks. Use whole milk—or nonfat milk if you prefer; low-fat milk doesn't froth up as well.

Here are the basic kinds of espresso-based drinks and the formulas for achieving them.

**Espresso Solo.** A single espresso, made with 1½ tablespoons of ground coffee through which about 1 ounce of hot water is passed.

**Espresso Doppio.** Literally, a double espresso, made with 3 tablespoons of ground coffee and 2 ounces of water.

**Espresso Ristretto.** A "restricted" espresso, made with the same amount of ground coffee as the solo, but with a little less water for a more concentrated shot.

**Espresso Macchiato.** A cup of espresso "marked" with a spoonful of the foam from steamed milk.

**Cappucino.** A double espresso topped with an equal volume each of steamed milk and milk foam. Named for the Capuchin order of monks, whose robe color the drink resembles.

**Caffe Latte.** A double espresso topped with up to twice the volume of steamed milk, plus a thin layer of foam.

**Latte Macchiato.** A cup of steamed milk "marked" with a small dash of espresso.

For a definitively Italian
taste sensation, try
dipping almond biscotti
into cups of just-brewed
espresso (right).

On the world-famous
Piazza San Marco,
Venice's Caffe Florian
(opposite page) has
served both citizens and
visitors since 1720.

### Almond Biscotti

The Italian word *biscotti* covers a wide range of crisp, sweet treats. This particular recipe combines coarsely chopped almonds with a tender-crisp butter cookie dough.

½ pound unsalted butter, at room temperature
⅔ cup granulated sugar
1 egg
¼ teaspoon vanilla extract
¼ teaspoon almond extract
2 cups all-purpose flour
½ cup coarsely chopped blanched almonds
½ teaspoon salt

In a mixing bowl or a processor fitted with the metal blade, cream together butter, sugar, egg, and extracts.

In a separate bowl, stir together flour, almonds, and salt. Gradually pulse dry ingredients into creamed mixture to form a smooth, firm dough. Form into a 12-inch-long log and wrap in waxed paper. Refrigerate at least 2 hours.

Preheat the oven to 375 degrees Fahrenheit.

Unwrap log and, with a small, sharp knife, slice into ¼-inch-thick rounds, placing them about 1 inch apart on ungreased baking sheets. Bake until light golden, 10 to 12 minutes; then transfer with a spatula to a wire rack to cool. Store in an airtight container. Makes about 4 dozen cookies.

### Espresso Granita

Since it does not require any kind of ice cream machine, this frozen dessert is very easy to make.

4 cups freshly brewed espresso coffee
6 tablespoons sugar
2 ounces dark chocolate, cut into thin shavings
  with a vegetable peeler

While espresso is still hot, stir together with sugar until sugar dissolves. Let cool to room temperature.

Pour coffee into metal ice cube trays without dividers, or into a metal baking pan. Freeze until ice crystals begin to form; stir with a fork and return to freezer. Continue freezing, stirring every 30 to 45 minutes, until mixture is very thick and scoopable.

Serve in chilled glasses or ice cream cups, topped with chocolate shavings. Makes 4 to 6 servings.

*Patrons enjoy newspapers, the morning sun, hot coffee, and the passing scene on the terrace of the Cafe de Flore in Paris.*

# Parisian *Cafe et Croissants*

"The finest beverage in the whole world," is how an un-identified turn-of-the-century travel writer described the morning coffee served to him in a Paris cafe. "The *garçon,* at your call for a *demitasse,* has placed before you a snowy cup and saucer, three lumps of sugar and a *petit verre.* He ventured the *petit verre,* inferring that you liked *liqueur.* Another *garçon* now appears; in his right hand is a huge silver pot, and in his left, another of the same material, uncovered: the former contains coffee—the latter, cream. You reject cream, and thereupon the *garçon* pours out of the former until your cup—aye, and almost the saucer— actually overflows. There is hardly space for the three lumps, and yet you must contrive, somehow, to insert them."

And the effects of that *cafe noir* upon our correspon-dent? "It agreeably affects several senses. Its liquid pleases all the gustatory nerves, its savour ascends to rejoice the olfactory, and even your eye is delighted with those dark, transparent, and sparkling hues, through which your sil-ver spoon perpetually shines. You pronounce French cof-fee the only coffee. In a few moments its miracles begin to be wrought; you feel *spirituel,* amiable, and conversa-tional."

It may be impossible to gauge precisely how much of the City of Light's fabled joie de vivre is attributable to the coffee served there, but any fan of French coffee would swear that the measure was significant.

*A plate of fine confectioner's chocolate truffles and a cup of just-brewed coffee are guaranteed to win a loved one's heart.*

The effect is also quite easy to achieve in one's own home, even with Paris thousands of miles away. All one needs is a good French-style dark roast of coffee, brewed fairly strong using whichever method one prefers. To start the day out right, pour it into large bowl-sized *cafe au lait* cups, mixing to taste almost equal parts of fresh-brewed coffee and hot milk. Serve with warm hunks of long, crusty French baguette—now widely available in good bakeries and supermarkets the world over. Buy or bake fresh, warm croissants, elaborated, perhaps, with a delightful filling of semisweet chocolate, jam, ham and cheese, or some other favorite breakfast ingredient.

Alongside the breakfast breads, present heavy, country crockery dishes of unsalted butter and chunky preserves.

Most good-sized metropolitan newsstands will carry copies of *Le Figaro,* the familiar Parisian daily, beloved of bistro habitués. Barring that, seek out some copies of the *International Herald Tribune,* to spark the fantasy that you're an English-speaking artist or writer living in Left Bank digs attempting to make your mark on European culture. Toss a blue pack of Gauloises cigarettes on the table for effect (far be it from me to suggest that you actually smoke them) and play a scratchy old Edith Piaf recording, to fully evoke an aura of "La Vie en Rose."

*Fresh-baked breakfast breads, cheeses, fresh fruit, and coffee provide a très élégant buffet-style continental breakfast.*

### Butter Croissants

You need to devote a little bit of time to this recipe, which is why it is best done as a weekend project—start on Saturday afternoon in order to serve at Sunday brunch.

**1 package active dry yeast**
**1 cup lukewarm milk (110–115 degrees Fahrenheit)**
**2½ cups all-purpose flour**
**2 teaspoons sugar**
**½ teaspoon salt**
**½ pound unsalted butter, softened**
**1 egg yolk**
**2 tablespoons water**

In a small bowl, dissolve yeast in a few tablespoons of milk. Stir in a few spoons of flour to make a soft, spongy mixture; cover and leave to rise at warm room temperature for 30 minutes.

In a mixing bowl, combine remaining flour with sugar and salt. Make a well in the center and add remaining warm milk, yeast sponge, and 4 tablespoons of the butter. With your fingers, gradually incorporate dry ingredients into wet to make a dough. Transfer to a floured work surface and knead by hand until smooth and elastic, about 5 minutes.

Return dough to a clean bowl, cover with plastic wrap, and let rise at warm room temperature until doubled in bulk, about 2 hours. Punch down dough in bowl, cover again, and leave in refrigerator to rise overnight.

The next morning, transfer dough to a cool, lightly floured work surface. With your hands, pat dough into a long rectangle about ½ inch thick. Spread remaining butter evenly over two thirds of rectangle's length. Fold unbuttered third over buttered middle third; then fold still-exposed buttered third on top, as if folding a letter. With your fingers, gently seal dough's edges.

Rotate dough 90 degrees on work surface. Dust a rolling pin with flour and lightly roll out dough again to its original rectangular shape. Fold into thirds once more, wrap in plastic, and refrigerate 1 hour.

Unwrap chilled dough, give another 90 degree turn, and roll and fold in thirds again. Repeat chilling, turning, rolling, and folding one final time, then rewrap and refrigerate 1 hour.

Unwrap dough and roll to a large rectangle about ⅛ inch thick. With a pastry cutter, cut dough into triangles with sides 5 to 6 inches long. Starting at one side, roll up each triangle; as you finish rolling, tuck the opposite point underneath and gently curve the ends inward to form a crescent shape.

Place croissants about 2 inches apart on a greased baking sheet. Cover with a kitchen towel and let rise at room temperature 1 hour.

Preheat oven to 375 degrees Fahrenheit. Lightly beat together egg yolk and water and brush over croissants. Bake until golden brown, 15 to 20 minutes. Makes about 1 dozen croissants.

# Filled Croissants

A basic croissant dough may be transformed into an even more delightful breakfast treat by adding just a touch of some imaginative filling.

Follow the instructions in the recipe for Butter Croissants, up to but not including the final cutting of the rolled-out dough into triangles. Instead, cut the dough into 6-inch squares. Place one of the fillings listed below across the central third of each square, stopping about ¼ inch short of the edge on each side. Fold the 2 sides over the filling, then pinch all open edges to seal. Let the croissants rise and bake them as in the basic recipe.

***Chocolate Croissants:*** Place a few small, broken pieces from a bittersweet chocolate bar across the center of each croissant.

***Ham-and-Cheese Croissants:*** Sprinkle in shredded Gruyère cheese and julienned strips of cooked ham.

***Jam Croissants:*** Spoon in 1 to 2 tablespoons of your favorite jam.

***Marzipan Croissants:*** Spread 1 tablespoon of prepared marzipan in each croissant, adding some jam if you like.

*Hot from the oven and accompanied by butter and preserves, a flaky croissant and its companion cup of coffee form the classic* petit dejeuner.

# British Elevenses

How easy it is to accept the notion that the British nation drinks tea, tea, more tea, and only tea. As the history of coffee amply bears out (see page 21), the United Kingdom has done as much as any nation to further the brew in its westward expansion. And although tea has, indeed, pushed its way into the number-one position in the hearts of most Britons, coffee remains a strong second. In the 1950s and 1960s, the rise of the beat generation and "swinging London" saw more than five hundred coffee bars serving espresso to denizens of the capital city. More recently, there has been a notable increase in boutique shops that sell highest-quality, freshly roasted beans.

That should come as no surprise to any Briton who looks forward to his or her "elevenses"—that mid-to-late-morning break meant to bridge the gap between the morning's breakfast and midday pub grub. Tea may well have roused the senses within moments of awakening; and it almost certainly will be the featured attraction come afternoon. But likely as not, the drink that accompanies elevenses will be a steaming mug of coffee.

For your own at-home elevenses, use clunky earthenware mugs and plates; or, for a more elegant occasion, use your finest china, preferably in a garden pattern. Set an informal table—in the sitting room, perhaps, or on the terrace if the weather is warm—with a pretty floral pattern or a crisp white linen cloth. To spark delightful conversation about things that *really* matter, place a few copies of *Majesty* or *Royalty* magazines discreetly nearby.

The trick to deciding what to serve at elevenses is in selecting a treat that is neither so savory nor so filling that it runs the risk of spoiling one's appetite for lunch. Nevertheless, it should satisfy and please the palate. A simple pound cake would do nicely, thank you very much, or a plate of good English biscuits—be they digestive biscuits, chocolate-orange Jaffa cakes, ginger snaps, or any of the other commercial products that have become long-standing British traditions.

As for the coffee itself, it stands to reason that one would want to select a variety from one of the former colonies. Kenyan coffee would do nicely, though one might also like to be a bit more daring and opt for the exotic choice of an Indian bean.

Remember, once you've broken with the traditional ties to tea, there's no telling where your unbridled wild streak might lead you.

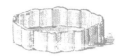

### Marmalade Pound Cake

In the traditional style that is the source of its name, this cake is made with a pound of each of its main ingredients. The addition of marmalade to the batter adds a delightful surprise to the finished cake's taste and texture.

**1 pound unsalted butter, softened**
**2 cups sugar**
**8 eggs, separated, whites beaten stiffly**
**½ cup thin-shred orange marmalade**
**1 tablespoon brandy**
**¼ teaspoon salt**
**4 cups cake flour**

Preheat the oven to 300 degrees Fahrenheit.

In a mixing bowl, cream together butter and sugar until light and fluffy. One at a time, beat in egg yolks until well blended. Beat in marmalade, brandy, and salt.

Gradually add and beat flour into other ingredients. Fold in beaten egg whites. Pour batter into 3 buttered and floured 8-inch loaf pans and bake until golden, springy to the touch, and a thin skewer or long wooden toothpick inserted into their centers comes out clean, about 1¼ hours. Makes 3 cakes.

### Fresh, Fresh, Fresh

"A JUG," SAID OLD MARGERY. "And would you be coming with me, Sir Deryck,—and softly,—whenever you have finished your breakfast."

"Softly," said Margery again, as they crossed the hall, the doctor's tall figure closely following in her portly wake. After mounting a few stairs she turned to whisper impressively: "It is not what ye make it *in*; it is *how* ye make it." She ascended a few more steps, then turned to say: "It all hangs upon the word *fresh*," and went on mounting. "Freshly roasted—freshly ground—water—freshly—boiled—" said old Margery, reaching the topmost stair somewhat breathless; then turning, bustled along a rather dark passage, thickly carpeted, and hung with old armour and pictures.

"Where are we going, Mistress Margery?" asked the doctor, adapting his stride to her trot—one to two.

"You will be seeing whenever we get there, Sir Deryck," said Margery. "And never touch it with metal, Sir Deryck. Pop it into an earthenware jug, pour your boiling water straight upon it, stir it with a wooden spoon, set it on the hob ten minutes to settle; the ground will all go to the bottom, though you might not think it, and you pour it out—fragrant, strong, and clear. But the secret is, fresh, fresh, fresh, and don't stint your coffee."

—Florence L. Barclay,
*The Rosary*

*Flowers from an English country garden complete the setting for a coffee table replete with dainty baked goods (page 84).*

*Who says you have to slave over a hot oven to throw a coffee party? A plate of bakery biscuits, lovingly selected and presented, sets the scene perfectly (left).*

# Dutch Morning Coffee Table

Coffee may well take on its most heartwarmingly homey aspect in the hands of the Dutch.

Go down to breakfast in the morning and bleary eyes are eased open with large, steaming cupfuls of wholesome-tasting coffee soothed by great lashings of warm milk—the Dutch version of cafe au lait. Indeed, the morning cupful may well have gained its particularly well-rounded flavor for having been "brewed" with a strong coffee extract—a concentrate that traces its lineage back to the old Dutch colonial island of Java.

And what accompanies that morning coffee? What else but a generous spread of simple foods that typify the honest fare of a country dairy farmhouse, even when served in the heart of the city: soft-boiled eggs kept warm in a napkin-lined basket, ready to be set in individual egg cups and gently cracked open; toasted slices of whole wheat and egg-enriched white bread; fresh-baked rolls and stacks of crunchy crispbreads; creamery butter, of course; and dishes of thick fruit preserves. And, of course, generous slices of Edam, Gouda, and Leyden cheeses, accompanied by thinly sliced ham and sausage.

For those who can't face quite so much food so early in the day, other options exist. Mid-morning, the milky cof-

*Cultivated rather than merely grown, coffee trees (opposite page) require careful tending—and their ripened fruit discerning picking.*

*Good bread, robust cheeses and sausages, boiled eggs, and other savory treats are the hallmarks of a generous Dutch coffee table (left).*

fee may be enjoyed with a plate of simple *koekjes*—little cookies. And the early morning farmhouse spread may well reappear at lunchtime, further elaborated into the *Hollandse koffietafel*—a "coffee table" of do-it-yourself sandwiches, adding perhaps simple roast beef slices, sliced hard-boiled eggs, and an easily prepared steak tartare mixture, along with pots of mayonnaise and mustard to moisten and flavor individual sandwiches to taste.

Whenever you serve it, give your own Dutch coffee spread a comforting aspect by choosing simple, country-style crockery, spread on an old lace tablecloth and augmented with Delftware platters, wooden carving boards, and serving baskets. Let the generous array of foods be the star: present cheeses, for example, in whole small wheels (Edam's red wax export covering is particularly attractive), and place cold cuts in neat overlapping patterns.

Most of all, make your welcome as warm as that traditionally offered to guests by a house-proud Dutch host. That, above all, will set the perfect tone for entertaining.

*In the Netherlands, a lunchtime coffee table could well include a hearty portion of* tartare biefstuk—*steak tartare.*

### Tartare Biefstuk

Offer this quick and simple classic as part of a Dutch *koffietafel*, accompanied by stacks of thinly sliced rye or pumpernickel bread.

**1 pound lean beef tenderloin, well-trimmed, cut into 1-to-2-inch chunks, and refrigerated**
**4 eggs, boiled in their shells 2 minutes, separated, whites discarded**
**¼ cup small capers, drained**
**¼ cup finely chopped sweet red onion**
**¼ cup finely chopped Italian parsley**
**2 tablespoons Worcestershire sauce**
**2 tablespoons salt**
**2 tablespoons freshly ground black pepper**
**¼ teaspoon hot pepper sauce**

In a food processor fitted with the metal blade, put beef chunks and process, pulsing machine on and off, until meat is finely and uniformly chopped.

Transfer meat to a mixing bowl and add egg yolks and remaining ingredients. Stir well with a fork to thoroughly but lightly blend mixture. Serve immediately. Makes about 2½ cups.

### Cafe au Lait à la Hollandaise

For a soothing cup of Dutch-style milky morning coffee, follow these simple instructions.

**1 cup whole or low-fat milk
1 to 2 tablespoons Dutch Coffee Concentrate**

In a saucepan over low heat, heat milk almost to boiling. Pour into a mug and stir in coffee concentrate to taste. Serve immediately. Makes 1 serving.

### Dutch Coffee Concentrate

Writer Francis B. Thurber described this method in 1881 in his book *Coffee from Plantation to Cup.*

**½ pound freshly ground medium-grind coffee
3 cups cold water**

In a large nonreactive glass or pottery jar, stir together coffee and water. Cover and leave to steep for 12 to 24 hours, depending on desired strength of final concentrate.

Line a good-sized funnel with a double thickness of filter cloth such as muslin or fine cheesecloth, and set inside a smaller jar. Pour coffee mixture into funnel. Let drain.

After filtering, cover and refrigerate the resulting concentrate, which will keep about 1 week.

To make coffee, fill a cup with freshly boiled water. Stir in 1 to 1½ tablespoons of concentrate, to taste. Makes about 2½ cups concentrate, enough for 28 to 40 cups.

### Speculaas *with Coffee Icing*

Spicy and crisp, these traditional Dutch cookies complement a cup of coffee wonderfully.

**2½ cups all-purpose flour
1 tablespoon baking powder
1 tablespoon ground cinnamon
1 teaspoon ground ginger
½ teaspoon grated nutmeg
½ teaspoon ground cloves
14 tablespoons unsalted butter
1¼ cups packed brown sugar
2½ tablespoons brandy
1 cup confectioners' sugar
2 teaspoons hot espresso coffee**

Preheat oven to 375 degrees Fahrenheit.

In a mixing bowl, stir together flour, baking powder, and spices. In a separate bowl, cream together butter and brown sugar until fluffy; stir in brandy.

Gradually beat dry ingredients into butter mixture, then form into a ball and knead on a floured surface until smooth. Roll out to a thickness of ¼ inch and cut with small cookie cutters, placing cutouts on a greased baking sheet.

Bake cookies until crisp and golden brown, 10 to 12 minutes. Transfer to a wire rack to cool.

For the icing, sift confectioners' sugar into a mixing bowl. A little at a time, stir in espresso with a fork. Rest bowl in a larger bowl of very hot tap water and stir about 1 minute, until icing is smooth and fluid. With a small knife or a teaspoon, spread a thin glaze of icing over each cookie and let set. Makes about 3 dozen cookies.

*A fresh fruit tart featuring summertime berries makes an outstanding seasonal addition to a Scandinavian-style* kaffeebord.

# Scandinavian Holiday *Kaffeebord*

Come the holiday season, hospitable folk throughout Scandinavia make coffee the linking element in a favorite form of entertaining: the *kaffeebord*. Just as the more widely familiar *smorrebord* or *smorgasbord* features a table (*bord*) of buttered sandwiches, so does the kaffeebord highlight coffee and all sorts of special baked goods and other delectables to go with it.

The dining table or sideboard will be set with the best linen or lace tablecloth and the most sparkling china. Candles cast their gentle, dancing glow across the festive array. There's plate after plate piled high with crisp, rich butter cookies—some subtly spiced, perhaps, and maybe decorated with dabs of jam or toasted nuts. Cakes, of course, will await being sliced and savored: a classic, buttery pound cake, most certainly, and the braided Finnish yeast cake known as *pulla*. Danes are likely to feature some version of what they call an apple cake—actually a puddinglike assemblage of applesauce and sweet bread crumbs.

Although the display of holiday treats is nothing short of glittering, the mood is nonetheless informal. Guests are invited to drop by over the course of the afternoon or during the evening, a time span specifically intended to indicate, subtly but surely, that dinner itself is not being served: 9 P.M. is not too late to begin the kaffeebord. Pots of mellow, medium-roast, blended coffee are freshly brewed at regular intervals and kept warm at table on a burner or hot plate turned low. Traditional carols play softly on the stereo in the background.

Though casual good humor reigns, Scandinavian social proprieties must still be observed with so many welcome guests in attendance. Take, for example, author Walter Bacon's description, in his book *Finland,* of how just such an occasion might proceed:

"Unassuming though this is, it is a mosaic of rules and procedures. The hostess announces that coffee is served, and the women advance towards it, the senior lady first. The men pretend not to have heard, or to be indifferent;

## Cardamom Crisps

A favorite spice in Scandinavia, cardamom adds a subtly exotic flavor to these crisp wafers.

**¼ pound unsalted butter**
**⅓ cup sugar**
**1 egg**
**2 teaspoons ground cardamom**
**1 teaspoon vanilla extract**
**⅛ teaspoon salt**
**¾ cup all-purpose flour**

Preheat oven to 375 degrees Fahrenheit.

In a mixing bowl, cream together butter and sugar. Beat in egg, cardamom, vanilla, and salt. Gradually beat in flour.

With a teaspoon, drop batter onto a greased cookie sheet 2 to 3 inches apart. Bake until edges are golden brown, about 10 minutes. Makes about 3 dozen.

### Appelkaka

Not truly a baked good, this Danish apple "cake" is traditionally made by layering sweetened and buttered bread crumbs with applesauce and whipped cream. In this version, crumbled pound cake is substituted for the bread crumbs, which saves the mess of mixing the crumbs with butter and sugar, while actually yielding a tastier result. Use the best applesauce you can buy, or your favorite homemade variety.

**5 cups plain unsweetened applesauce**
**½ cup brown sugar**
**1 tablespoon ground cinnamon**
**1 teaspoon lemon juice**
**½ teaspoon ground allspice**
**½ teaspoon ground cloves**
**½ teaspoon grated nutmeg**
**5 cups coarsely crumbled pound cake**
**1 cup whipping cream, chilled**
**1 teaspoon confectioner's sugar**
**1 teaspoon vanilla extract**

In a large mixing bowl, stir together applesauce, brown sugar, and spices. Spread one third of the cake crumbs in the bottom of a 3-quart glass casserole; spread half the applesauce mixture on top. Repeat with another third of crumbs and all remaining applesauce. Cover evenly with remaining crumbs.

Before serving, beat cream until thick. Add sugar and vanilla and continue beating until soft peaks form. Mound cream attractively on top of casserole. Makes about 12 servings.

they are actually wondering who is the senior man. (In the countryside, a clergyman would take precedence over everyone.) After the first cup, no one ever says, 'May I have another cup of your delicious coffee?' Instead they wait till the hostess walks round with the coffee pot; after this the party advances on the table in the same order as before."

And that procedure may well be repeated over and over again, until each guest has consumed as many as five steaming cupfuls and plate after plate of holiday treats.

*Kona coffee berries (opposite page) cluster on the branch of a tree on a plantation near Captain Cook, Hawaii.*

*Topped with vanilla-flavored whipped cream, an individual bowl of Danish* appelkaka *(left), a pudding of pound cake crumbs and spiced applesauce, tempts the palate.*

*Coffeehouse patrons enjoy their brew beneath the Alster arcades across from the city hall in Hamburg, Germany.*

# The German *Kaffeeklatsch*

More than a century ago, Mark Twain had a few choice, barbed observations to make about how German coffee might be made:

> Take a barrel of water and bring it to a boil; rub a chicory berry against a coffee berry, then convey the former into the water. Continue the boiling and evaporation until the intensity of the flavor and aroma of the coffee and chicory has been diminished to a proper degree . . . then set aside to cool.

Twain's cockeyed sense of humor and distrust of things not resoundingly American almost certainly found German coffee guilty and sentenced it to death without a trial. The fact of the matter is, you can most certainly get an excellent cup of coffee in Germany today—as you probably could in Twain's time.

Indeed, good coffee is essential to that most German of social institutions: the *Kaffeeklatsch*. The term was originally coined in the nineteenth century, by male wags no doubt, to describe the clatter of gossip and scandal that ensued when German women got together over their afternoon cup. Its meaning has since broadened to convey the relaxed, delightful conversation to be had over coffee—whether served at home or in one of the nation's fabled *Konditoreien*, or pastry shops.

An invitation to friends to join you for late-afternoon coffee is one of the most highly valued social niceties in Germany. The occasion calls for a table set with your finest heirloom service—including, should you have it, beautiful old Meissen pottery. No self-respecting host or hostess would present a table without a fine lace tablecloth and at least one vase of fresh flowers. *Schön decken*—setting a beautiful table—is still a valued skill. And that beautiful setting will most certainly include dainty cookies and pieces of cake. (It's okay to stop at the best local bakery if you don't have the time to make them yourself.) For a really special *Kaffee,* you might want to supplement the array of foods with a tray of open-faced finger sandwiches.

The coffee itself should not have a trace of the chicory that Mark Twain so abhorred in the German coffee he drank. Choose a blend of beans that is rich and mellow, and roasted perhaps a touch darker than you're used to (which may well explain the slight bitter edge to which the humorist overreacted). Transfer the coffee to a china pot for serving, and cover it with a cozy to keep the brew hot. Serve fresh cream for guests to pour into the coffee, even though German custom often dictates that the cream be canned—a taste some folk still inexplicably prefer. And, for an extra-gracious touch, offer glasses of brandy with the final cup of coffee.

As important as anything else you might serve, the conversation offered up should be the best you can muster. *Kaffee,* after all, is an opportunity to while away the few remaining hours of daylight in the most pleasant of company, to review the day's events, to catch up on the news, and to philosophize.

And yes, it *is* a time to gossip in the best *Kaffeeklatsch* tradition.

*Dainty yet robust-tasting open-faced sandwiches whet the appetite for a German afternoon Kaffee.*

### German **Kaffee** *Sandwiches*

For an afternoon *Kaffee* at which you would like to impress a special guest, offer a platter of these little finger sandwiches before the sweet treats get passed.

**12 thin slices (about 4 x 4 inches) packaged German brown bread or pumpernickel**
**¼ pound (1 stick) unsalted butter, softened**
**12 canned anchovy fillets, drained, rinsed, and patted dry**
**1 tablespoon German mustard**
**6 ounces high-quality German liverwurst**
**6 hard-boiled eggs, cut into ¼-inch-thick slices**
**½ cup finely chopped fresh parsley**

With a bread knife, neatly trim crusts from bread slices. Stack a few slices at a time and cut in thirds to make fingers.

In a shallow bowl, use a fork to first mash one third of the butter, then mix it with the anchovies to make a smooth paste. Spread neatly on 12 bread fingers. Set aside.

Spread remaining butter on remaining 24 bread fingers. Thinly spread mustard on 12 of them and then spread these neatly with liverwurst. Set aside.

Neatly array egg slices on remaining buttered bread fingers.

Garnish each finger sandwich with chopped parsley. Arrange each kind of sandwich neatly on a serving plate; or arrange all together on a larger platter. Makes 3 dozen sandwiches, about 12 servings.

## Honey Ginger Cake

A simple, elegant sponge cake such as this may well be served along with store-bought cookies for a casual midweek *Kaffee*. Etiquette dictates that the cake be cut into small pieces.

**1 cup self-raising flour**
**1 tablespoon ground ginger**
**2 teaspoons finely grated lemon zest**
**1 teaspoon unsweetened cocoa powder**
**½ teaspoon baking powder**
**¼ teaspoon salt**
**1½ tablespoons unsalted butter, softened**
**6 tablespoons honey, at room temperature**
**¼ cup packed brown sugar**
**2 eggs, beaten**

Preheat oven to 350 degrees Fahrenheit.

In a mixing bowl, stir together flour, ginger, lemon zest, cocoa, baking powder, and salt. With your fingers, rub butter into mixture until it forms crumbs. Make a well in center, add remaining ingredients, and beat with a wooden spoon until smooth, about 2 minutes.

Grease a 7 x 7-inch cake pan, line with parchment or waxed paper, and pour in batter. Bake until top is firm and a cake tester inserted into center comes out clean, about 30 minutes. Remove from pan and cool on wire rack. Cut in half, then cut halves crosswise into ½-inch slices. Makes 28 slices, 12 to 14 servings.

# The Viennese Cafe Scene

More than the Royal Lipizzaner stallions or the famed boys' choir. More than the home of Beethoven, Brahms, Haydn, Liszt, Mozart, Schubert, Strauss (both father and son), and Wagner. More than St. Stephan's Church, the Hofburg and Belvedere palaces, and the Prater Ferris wheel forever enshrined in Orson Welles' *The Third Man*.

More than all these justifiably beloved sights, the very soul of Vienna may be found in its cafes, which embody all the warmth, the charm, the coziness . . . the *Gemutlichkeit* of Viennese life. Enter one of the city's older establishments and you feel transported back to the turn of the century. You're in a public palace of marble floors, crystal chandeliers, and walls adorned with polished wood and mirrors. The tables are covered with crisp white linens.

A waiter—clad in a tuxedo or a white serving jacket—greets you as if he knows and respects you. He leads you to your table, past one of the essential features of a Viennese cafe, the newspaper rack. Clipped to long wooden sticks are the papers of the day—not just those of Vienna but also often from other major European cities. There are news magazines as well, along with journals on fashion, cooking, and sports.

Already, you begin to understand that this is more than just a place for a snack, it's a retreat at which you can refresh your mind, your heart, and your very soul.

It's so easy to get absorbed in your own thoughts here that you don't notice the passage of time. A local humorist once remarked that the Viennese cafe is "the ideal place for people who want to be alone but need company to do it." Many locals treat cafes as their personal clubs—writing letters, receiving mail, and even conducting meetings there. No wonder, then, that certain cafes have come to be associated with particular professions. Cafe Landtmann (once a favorite of Sigmund Freud) is favored by actors from the neighboring Burgtheater. Artists and intellectuals gravitate toward the Cafe Hawelka. And close by the State Opera House are two of the city's loveliest, most lyrical cafes: the Mozart and the Sacher.

Cafe Sacher is the ideal spot for sampling Vienna's glorious pastries—most notably the *Sachertorte*, a dense chocolate sponge cake layered with apricot jam and coated with thick, bittersweet chocolate icing. Other delicacies served both here and elsewhere include fruit strudels; the almond-paste-and-raspberry *Linzertorte*; the seven-layer, caramel-topped spongecake-and-chocolate-cream *Doboschtorte*; and any number of other tempting and delightfully rich creations.

Fortunately, you don't need a Ph.D. in pastry to recreate the Viennese experience at home: most Continental-style bakeries throughout the world regularly offer Linzertorte and strudels at the very least, and a not-too-strenuous search could well turn up a Doboschtorte or even a Sachertorte.

Launder and starch your best white linens for the table, and polish up a silver—or at least stainless steel—coffee service for pouring a classic Viennese blend. Whip up plenty of cream until it forms voluptuously soft peaks, adding (only if you must) just the barest hint of confectioner's sugar. Have a sturdy glass pitcher filled with ice water at the ready, to be poured into small juice glasses. Array

*Simple, elegant appointments—silver tray, sugar bowl and creamer, crisp linens, and sturdy china—can turn a simple cup of coffee into a special occasion.*

the latest international newspapers and magazines on a nearby table for your guests to thumb through and discuss.

Then set some Strauss waltzes on the stereo and let the music begin!

### Linzertorte

Rich and satisfying though it tastes, there's something wonderfully pure and simple about this classic pastry from the Austrian town of Linz. An almond-flavored crust spread with raspberry jam, topped with another pastry lattice, and then baked, it looks like a wonderfully elaborate example of the pastry-maker's art; yet its preparation is surprisingly easy.

Cut it into wedges like a pie, to be eaten with knife and fork.

**1½ cups all-purpose flour**
**1 cup ground almonds**
**½ cup sugar**
**2 teaspoons finely grated lemon zest**
**1 teaspoon ground cinnamon**
**½ pound unsalted butter, softened**
**2 egg yolks, lightly beaten**
**1 teaspoon kirsch**
**1 teaspoon vanilla extract**
**¼ cup raspberry jam, at room temperature**
**1 whole egg, lightly beaten**

In a mixing bowl, stir together flour, almonds, sugar, lemon zest, and cinnamon. Make a well in the center and add butter, egg yolks, kirsch, and vanilla. Beat well with a wooden spoon until a smooth dough forms. Gather into a ball, wrap in plastic wrap, and refrigerate 1 hour.

Preheat oven to 350 degrees Fahrenheit.

Butter a 9-inch round tart pan with removable bottom. Remove about ¾ of the dough from refrigerator and, with your hands, press into tart pan to line its bottom and side evenly. Spread jam evenly onto bottom of pie shell.

*(continued on page 102, column 1)*

*(continued from page 101, column 2)*

On a floured surface, use a rolling pin to roll out remaining dough to a thickness of about ¼ inch. With a fluted or plain pastry wheel or cutter, cut dough into strips about ½ inch wide. Lay strips across top of tart to form a lattice pattern. With your fingertips, pinch ends of strips against side of crust dough to seal.

Brush pastry with beaten egg. Bake until golden, about 45 minutes. Cool to room temperature before serving in thin wedges. Makes about 12 servings.

## Viennese Coffee Options

WITH TYPICAL EXUBERANCE AND EXCESS, the Viennese have transformed coffee into much more than the brew that other people around the world enjoy. Today's cafes allow you to enjoy their inventiveness in more than a dozen different coffee drinks. A *Schwarze* is black coffee, available *grosse* (large cup) or *kleine* (small). A *Kapuziner* is the local variation on the familiar cappucino, in which a tiny splash of milk is added to regular brewed coffee. Add more milk, and you progress through the *Schale braun* ("brown bowl") to the *Schale gold* and *Schale licht* ("light"), not to mention the very popular *Melange* (a mix of two-thirds coffee and one-third hot milk). Then there's the *Einspanner,* fancifully named after a one-horse cab: coffee in a tall glass, topped with *Schlag,* the luscious Viennese whipped cream.

You can, in fact, order any of these creations *mit Schlag* or even *mit Doppelschlag* (a double portion). The cream will arrive in its own little bowl on your serving tray, along with coffee's traditional accompaniments here: a tiny dish of sugar cubes and a short glass of cold water.

Though there are no automatic coffee refills, there are on the water, which has led to a certain type of cafe customer known as a *Drei Wasser.* He's the one who, settled in with a single cup of coffee and a newspaper, spends the entire afternoon taking up a seat while the waiter brings one, then another, then a third glass of water to the table.

*A newspaper, just-baked pastries, and freshly brewed coffee make morning in Vienna complete (opposite page).*

*The classic Austrian accompaniment to afternoon coffee: a slice of raspberry-and-almond Linzertorte (left).*

# COFFEE OCCASIONS IN THE NEW WORLD & BEYOND

*J*ust as coffee ventured forth from the Old World to conquer the New, so did the occasions that accompany it. Apart from its beguiling aroma and flavor and its eye-opening powers, coffee has a knack for winning converts that has a lot to do with its adaptability. From Latin America to the United States to Asia, every nation that has taken coffee to its table and its heart has, in some subtle yet real way, made the drink its own.

# Brazilian Day-Long Coffee

Throughout Latin America, coffee is the reigning beverage—a distinction well-earned by the ruling export crop. Wherever you go in large cities or small towns, coffee's aroma seems almost to linger in the air.

Brazilians are probably Latin America's most delightfully self-indulgent coffee drinkers. Each citizen's morning usually begins with a large cup of *cafe com leite:* half coffee brewed to almost double strength, in the prevailing Latin American fashion; half hot milk; and a few generous teaspoons of sugar. At once gentle and rousing, it is the perfect start to a day of truly serious coffee drinking that may see at least twenty cups consumed before head hits pillow once again. In Rio, for example, homes, shops, offices, and streets carry a steady traffic of people carrying metal trays filled with small porcelain cups and saucers, bowls of sugar, and pots of coffee, ever delivering the king elixir to its waiting subjects.

For a Brazilian coffee hour in your own home—to be served any time of day, but preferably late in the morning or early in the afternoon—place your best little white cups and saucers on a silver or stainless steel tray. Brew your coffee—made from Brazilian beans, of course—in proportions of at least three tablespoons (45 ml) of ground coffee to every six ounces (19ml) of hot water. For guests to whom the resulting brew might seem overwhelming, offer a small pot of hot water on the side for the purpose of dilution. Set out a sugar bowl well-filled with white or

*With coffee on the menu, any occasion promises to be rich and satisfying (page 104).*

*Arranged in neat rows for easier harvesting, coffee trees stretch off into the distance on a coffee estate in Curitiba, Brazil (right).*

*Brazilian tropical treats bring out coffee's seductively exotic qualities.*

light brown sugar. As an accompaniment, pass around a plate of sweets that capture the tropical taste of Brazil—coconut cookies flavored with pineapple, for example.

The standard way for you or your guests to drink a Brazilian *cafezhino* is to almost fill a demitasse with sugar—three or four small demitasse spoons would be moderate. Then pour strong coffee over it and savor the black, syrupy liquid with relish and gusto—after all, you'll probably be consuming another one in less than thirty minutes. Indeed, come cocktail hour, you may well want to forego the regular hot brew and instead mix up a *batida*—a cocktail based on *cachaca,* the local rum, some-times flavored with the favorite local brew. It's just the thing to sip as you listen to the swaying sounds of the music of Antonio Carlos Jobim.

### Brazilian Coffee Batida

The word *batida* is Portuguese for "beaten," which perfectly describes the vigorous preparation of this frothy, rum-based cocktail.

**3 teaspoons sugar**
**½ cup cold, strong Brazilian coffee**
**2 shots rum**
**2 egg whites**

Moisten the rims of 2 cocktail glasses and dip and turn in 1 teaspoon of sugar to coat. Set aside.

Put remaining sugar, coffee, rum, and egg whites in a cocktail shaker filled with cracked ice. Close and shake vigorously to blend, until mixture is frothy.

Strain into prepared cocktail glasses and serve immediately. Makes 2 servings.

### Coconut-Pineapple Pyramids

These macaroon-like confections have the added tropical flourish of chopped dried pineapple—a rich and tangy combination that nicely offsets a sharp, sweet cup of Brazilian coffee.

**1 cup packed brown sugar**
**1 cup packed shredded coconut**
**¼ cup finely chopped dried or candied pineapple**
**1½ tablespoons unsalted butter, melted**
**4 teaspoons honey**
**1 tablespoon pineapple jam**
**4 egg whites**

Preheat oven to 350 degrees Fahrenheit.

In a mixing bowl, beat egg whites until stiff; add remaining ingredients and stir until well mixed.

Spoon heaping tablespoons of mixture onto a baking sheet lined with waxed paper or parchment paper. Bake until golden, about 20 minutes. Makes about 2 dozen.

# Mexican Morning Coffee

The native drink of Mexico, chocolate is a noble brew whose use dates back to the fabled court of Moctezuma. But coffee, day in and day out, holds its own today as the daytime drink of the common man; who, after all, could down cup after cup of cocoa after every single meal, no matter how hallowed chocolate's place in history may be?

Nevertheless, Mexicans have succeeded in making coffee a drink entirely their own. Mexican coffee beans themselves are often roasted with sugar to produce a dark caramel finish that actually causes them to stick together when cool and gives a bittersweet edge to the daily cupful. Often, they'll grind a little cinnamon stick with the beans to add an extra spark to the brew. And by mixing spice, sugar, and a hint of fruit with coffee specially prepared in an *olla,* an earthenware pot, they make a beverage that is as delightfully lively and ingratiating as the music of a mariachi band.

Serve your Mexican coffee—whether plain, cinnamon-spiked, or elaborately prepared in an olla—in sturdy, brightly painted earthenware pots. Offer soft brown sugar to sweeten the brew and add a hint of richness. Decorate the table with a colorfully embroidered tablecloth and some bright-hued flowers; tissue-paper flowers, fashioned with your own hands or bought from a local crafts stall, add their own festive air. Of course, you'll want a hint of Mexican music: for daytime, mariachi, played loud enough for its impact to be enjoyed but not so loud as to

conflict with conversation; at night, some of the stirring Mexican ballads known as *corridos,* whether an imported album or the excellent renditions on Linda Ronstadt's *Canciones de mi Padre.*

At breakfast time, serve the coffee with fresh, plain tortillas, sweet tamales, or the deep-fried pastries known as *churros*; these are all widely available in Mexican markets and bakeries. After dinner, serve it with a classic Mexican flan—a smooth, creamy egg custard that will highlight the coffee's natural richness.

And enjoy it *con mucho gusto!*

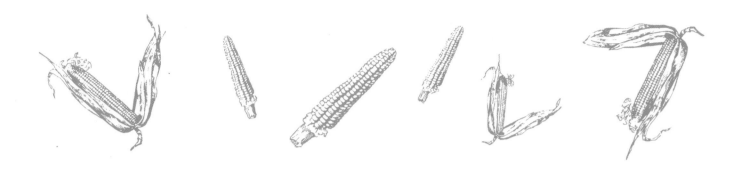

### Sweet Breakfast Tamales

Tamales are, in essence, cornmeal dumplings steamed in corn husks. Usually, they are the base for a savory lunch or dinner main course. But in the recipe that follows, they've been simplified and lightly sweetened as a satisfying breakfast dish.

**14 large dried corn husks**
**2 cups masa harina**
**1 tablespoon sugar**
**½ tablespoon salt**
**1¼ teaspoons baking powder**
**⅓ cup solid vegetable shortening**
**3 tablespoons unsalted butter, softened**
**1 cup milk**
**2 small ears fresh corn, kernels removed**
**12 tablespoons golden seedless raisins**

Put corn husks and add lukewarm water to cover in the sink or a large bowl. Soak for at least 5 minutes.

Meanwhile, in a mixing bowl or a food processor fitted with the metal blade, combine masa harina, sugar, salt, and baking powder. Add shortening and butter and mash, using a pastry cutter or fork or pulsing processor, until mixture resembles fine crumbs. Add milk and stir or process to form a soft paste. Stir in corn kernels.

Drain corn husks and tear 2 lengthwise into ¼- to ½-inch-wide strips. In center of a whole husk, place 2 tablespoons masa harina mixture, spreading into a rectangle about ½ inch thick and 1 x 3 inches wide. Sprinkle 1 tablespoon raisins in center. Top with 2 more tablespoons masa harina mixture, patting edges to enclose raisins.

Fold up top and bottom of corn husk, then fold in sides, to enclose masa harina mixture completely; tie securely across middle with a strip of corn husk. Repeat with remaining husks, masa, and raisins.

In a vegetable steamer, bring several inches of water to a boil. Place tamales in steamer basket, cover, and cook about 45 minutes. Remove from steamer and let cool about 5 minutes before serving. Let guests unwrap individual tamales. Makes 12 tamales, 6 servings.

*A young country boy gains a loftier vantage point by becoming king of the mountain on a pile of coffee bean bags (page 110).*

*Surrounded by a pool of delicate caramel syrup, smooth, satisfying flan (right) goes beautifully with a cup of rich dark coffee.*

### Mexican Vanilla Bean Flan

**1 cup sugar**
**½ cup water**
**1 cup whipping cream**
**1 cup milk**
**1 whole vanilla bean, carefully split lengthwise**
  **with a small, sharp knife**
**3 eggs**
**2 egg yolks**
**½ cup packed brown sugar**
**Pinch of salt**

For the caramel, put sugar and water in a small saucepan and bring to a boil over moderate heat, stirring until sugar dissolves. Continue boiling, without stirring, until syrup turns medium golden brown, 5 to 7 minutes. Immediately remove from heat and divide equally among 6 individual custard cups, turning each cup to coat bottom and sides evenly.

For the custard, put cream and milk in a medium saucepan over moderate heat. As soon as liquid is hot and begins to bubble along sides, remove from heat. Scrape vanilla seeds into liquid. Stir well.

Meanwhile, in a mixing bowl, lightly beat eggs, egg yolks, sugar, and salt with a small whisk.

Preheat oven to 325 degrees Fahrenheit. Bring a kettle of water to a boil.

Stirring continuously with whisk, slowly pour 6 ounces of hot milk into egg mixture. Pour back into remaining milk and stir to blend.

Distribute flan mixture evenly among reserved caramel-coated cups. Put cups in a shallow baking

*(continued on page 114, column 1)*

*(continued from page 113, column 2)*

pan. Open the oven, pull out a shelf, and place pan on it; then carefully pour boiling water into baking pan to come halfway up sides of custard cups. Carefully slide shelf back into oven.

Bake until a small, sharp knife inserted into the center of a flan comes out clean, 20 to 25 minutes. Cool to room temperature, then refrigerate.

Before serving, run a knife around edge of each flan to loosen. Place an upside-down serving plate over a cup and, holding them together, invert, shaking downward slightly to unmold flan. Carefully lift away cup before serving. Makes 6 servings.

## Cafe de Olla

Use a heavy, heatproof earthenware jug for brewing this coffee in traditional fashion.

**6 tablespoons coarsely ground,
  dark-roasted coffee
¼ cup packed brown sugar
4 whole cinnamon sticks
4 whole cloves
1 small orange, thinly sliced
4 cups freshly boiled water**

Put ground coffee, sugar, cinnamon, cloves, and orange slices in jug. Pour water into jug, stir with a wooden spoon, cover, and let steep 10 minutes.

Pour coffee through a small strainer into large heated mugs. Makes 4 servings.

*Orange peel and sweet spices add intrigue to Mexican-style cafe de olla.*

### *Corn Tortillas*

Though you can buy decent tortillas in most supermarkets today, nothing beats the wonderfully earthy flavor of those you make by hand from the prepared tortilla flour—*masa harina*—also sold in the flour section of supermarkets.

Eat these hot off the griddle, spread evenly with butter or jam.

**2 cups masa harina**
**¼ teaspoon salt**
**1 to 1¼ cups warm water**

In a mixing bowl, stir together masa harina and salt. Stir in enough water to make a thick, firm, but still soft dough.

Heat a cast-iron griddle or heavy skillet over moderate-to-high heat.

Divide dough into 12 equal balls. Using your lightly moistened hands, a rolling pin, or a cast-iron tortilla press lined with waxed paper, pat or press a ball into a tortilla about 6 inches in diameter. Place on the hot griddle and cook until it just begins to turn golden brown and its edges curl, 1 to 1½ minutes per side. Transfer to a napkin-lined basket while cooking remaining tortillas. Makes 1 dozen.

*Coffee beans in a holding tank before being spread out to dry (opposite page).*

*The spirit of Mardi Gras prevails year-round in two of New Orleans' most beloved specialties— chicory-laced coffee and sugar-dusted beignets (right).*

*Day or night, the Cafe du Monde (page 119) in New Orleans provides locals and tourists with outstanding coffee and beignets.*

# Coffee, *Beignets*, & the Devil's Brew in New Orleans' *Vieux Carré*

Any time of the day or night, wander down to the Mississippi where it borders the *Vieux Carré*—the heart of old New Orleans—and you'll experience the ultimate in American coffee drinking. On the open-air terrace of the fabled Cafe du Monde, you'll join dozens of other locals and tourists, all savoring steaming cups of sharp, chicory-laced Louisiana-style coffee, served with the deep-fried and sugar-dusted pastries known as *beignets*, the perfect object for dunking.

For some, sharp and somewhat bitter chicory coffee is an acquired taste; for the citizens of New Orleans, however, the drink is steeped in tradition, tracing its roots back to the Civil War, when coffee was scarce and had to be eked out with that most prevalent of substitutes. Now they prefer their coffee that way—and you might too, once you've enjoyed a morning cup of the local *cafe au lait*, in which the strong black coffee is mixed with an equal quantity of hot, rich milk that seems to polish the chicory's rough edges. It's worth a try; many coffee stores still offer blends with chicory, and you can also buy the blend—along with the Cafe du Monde's classic batter mix for *beignets*—from a number of mail-order firms specializing in foods of the region (see Appendix).

Another way to learn to love New Orleans–style coffee is in one of the classic after-dinner drinks that have evolved into world-renowned classics over the years in the city's finer restaurants. Savor a Cafe Royale or a Cafe Diable—the devil's own coffee—and you may well feel as if you've given over your very soul to the brew.

Whatever time of day you serve your coffee, never forget the city's French roots; get out your finest porcelain and silver to set a truly glittering table. Then add a touch of New Orleans' own distinctive culture with a record of classic Dixieland jazz played by the Preservation Hall Band, some good Cajun zydeco music, or, for a more con-

temporary touch, an album of songs by the city's own Harry Connick, Jr.

With such sounds stirring your soul, coffee—even if you never liked chicory before—will never have tasted sweeter.

### New Orleans Beignets

Though the following recipe is fairly easy, if you don't want to go to the trouble of mixing the batter from scratch, New Orleans' Cafe du Monde markets an excellent mix.

1 cup all-purpose flour
1 teaspoon sugar
½ teaspoon salt
1 cup cold water
¼ pound unsalted butter, cut into ½-inch pieces
4 eggs, lightly beaten
Vegetable oil for deep frying
Confectioners' sugar

Sift flour, sugar, and salt together onto a sheet of waxed paper. Set aside.

In a saucepan, heat water and butter together over low heat, then raise heat to moderate and bring to a boil. Remove from heat, carefully lift up waxed paper from opposite sides, and lift and pour flour mixture into pan. Stir vigorously with a wooden spoon until a smooth paste forms. Return to moderate heat and continue stirring until dough pulls away from side of pan. Remove from heat and let cool about 5 minutes.

In 4 separate additions, beat eggs vigorously into dough until mixture is smooth and shiny.

While dough is still warm, in a large heavy skillet or deep fryer, heat several inches of oil to 375 degrees Fahrenheit on a deep-frying thermometer. Dip a tablespoon in hot oil and use to scoop dough, carefully dropping it into oil from close to the surface; repeat, adding only enough spoonfuls to avoid overcrowding skillet. Fry until puffed and golden brown, turning several times for even cooking, about 6 minutes total. Drain well on paper towels.

Serve hot, dusted to taste with confectioners' sugar. Makes about 2 dozen beignets.

### Cafe Royale

This classic after-dinner presentation could not be simpler to prepare.

**3 ounces freshly brewed strong black coffee**
**1 teaspoon sugar**
**1 teaspoon brandy or cognac**

Pour hot coffee into a demitasse. In a metal tablespoon, combine sugar and brandy. Light a match and carefully touch to side of spoon to ignite brandy. When flames just begin to die down, pour into demitasse and serve. Makes 1 serving.

### Cafe Diable

Also known as Cafe Brulot, this devilishly good drink is—in essence—a kind of mulled coffee.

**½ cup brandy**
**2 tablespoons sugar**
**5 whole cloves**
**4 6-inch strips orange peel**
**4 3-inch strips lemon peel**
**2 2-inch pieces cinnamon stick**
**2 1-inch pieces vanilla bean**
**4 cups strong black coffee**

Put all ingredients, except coffee, in a chafing dish. Warm gently, stirring until sugar dissolves and brandy is warm. Light brandy and let it burn for about 30 seconds, then ladle mixture into cups three quarters full of hot coffee. Makes 4 servings.

*Ripe Caribbean fruits (right) provide soothing contrast to the full-bodied, mildly acidy, mellow flavor of Jamaican Blue Mountain coffee.*

# Jamaican Afternoon Coffee Beside Blue Mountain

The Blue Mountains of Jamaica, which are north of Kingston, produce some of the world's most renowned coffee beans, prized for their rich, full flavor and light acidity. But high-mountain-grown Blue Mountain is a rarity, and much more coffee gets sold—at prices sometimes twice as much, or more, than other beans—under that label in a year than is actually produced there; so buy it from a reputable dealer.

Once you do, make the brewing of Blue Mountain an occasion to serve an island-style afternoon cup of coffee. Capture the Caribbean influence by setting out platters of sweet, ripe tropical fruits: mango, papaya, pineapple, all chilled, sliced, and presented with bowls of shredded and toasted coconut and wedges of lime for guests to sprinkle or squeeze over the fruit to taste. The tangy, exotically perfumed, and sweet fruit contrasts remarkably well with a good cup of coffee. For another unusual, island-style nibble, you might wish to offer a bowl of banana chips; eaten like potato chips, they make a surprising savory-sweet snack. Want to go even more exotic? Then offer around small glasses of the island's favorite Tia Maria or your own homemade coffee liqueur.

Reflecting the island's rich colonial heritage, which exhibits Spanish, French, and English influences, go all out on your presentation, using your best European-style coffee service. But don't hesitate to add a touch of Caribbean flair: some brightly colored linens, some outrageous flowers, a few potted palms strategically positioned to sway in a real or artificial breeze—and certainly some reggae music pulsing softly in the background. To while away a sultry afternoon as the islanders might, set out an old, well-worn set of dominoes; even if you don't know the rules, the feel of the pieces and the gentle clack as they touch the table and each other are hypnotic.

The more deeply you fall under the island's spell, the less likely you are to feel the pain of shelling out so much money for that Blue Mountain coffee.

## Homemade Coffee-Rum Liqueur

The manufacturers of the world's great liqueurs jealously guard their formulas, and with good reason: the best liqueurs are made from old traditional formulas that are the result of years and years of careful trial and error.

But it is possible to prepare your own simple liqueur at home using commercial liquor and roasted coffee beans. Give it a try, and see how you like it.

**3 cups light rum**
**1½ cups dark-roasted whole Jamaican coffee**
　**beans**
**½ vanilla bean pod**
**½ cup sugar**

In a sterilized quart bottle, combine all ingredients, adding sugar to taste. Cap securely and store away from light at cool room temperature.

After 1 week, sip a little to see if the coffee flavor suits your taste; leave beans to infuse up to 1 week longer, until desired strength is reached. Then strain liqueur into a decanter, cover, and store.

Serve in liqueur glasses, or use as a topping for ice cream. Makes about 1½ pints.

## Banana Chips

Choose the *least ripe* bananas you can find in your supermarket: the firmer they are, the more neatly they'll slice and the more crisply they'll fry.

**Vegetable oil for deep frying**
**1 pound firm, underripe bananas**
**Salt (optional)**
**Hot paprika (optional)**

In a large heavy skillet or deep fryer, heat several inches of oil to 375 degrees Fahrenheit on a deep-frying thermometer. While oil is heating, peel bananas and cut crosswise into slices as thin as potato chips.

Carefully scatter a small handful of chips into oil, separating slices as you do; avoid overcrowding skillet. Fry until golden, turning occasionally with a wire skimmer or slotted spoon, about 4 minutes total. Remove with slotted spoon or skimmer and drain well on paper towels.

If you like, sprinkle to taste with salt; for a more exotic, spicier effect, dust lightly with paprika as well. Makes about 2 cups.

*Two children find a hideout from the tropical heat and humidity of a coffee plantation.*

*On a hillside Indian coffee estate, tall trees provide the requisite shade for the young coffee trees that grow beneath them (right).*

*A worker harvests coffee berries on an Indian plantation (opposite page).*

# Afternoon Coffee Time in Southern India

Although most people think of India as a tea-drinking nation, the love of coffee is heartily sustained there—particularly in the south—by a buoyant coffee-growing industry. Some five hundred years ago, so legend would have it, an Arabian pilgrim named Baba Buden carried a coffee plant to the city of Mysore; that tree's offspring were in turn carried to neighboring regions, where their cultivation and brewing grew together. Today, northern Indians indeed drink their tea, as all the world imagines them doing; but to the south, the locally grown coffee is the drink of choice.

And, served throughout the day either on its own with a few little nibbles, or accompanying a meal, it makes an ideal complement to the hot, largely vegetarian dishes of southern India. Many households take coffee as the very first food after waking. Freshly roasted and finely ground, it is mixed with raw palm sugar—known locally as "jaggery"—and boiled in water, then enriched with milk. Come breakfast time, it is served once more with steamed coconut-and-rice cakes, the pancakes known as *dosai,* and sweet-tart fruit chutney.

Coffee also follows the main midday meal. And late in the afternoon—traditional tea time—it is coffee time in southern India, as the brew is served with an array of sweet and spicy tidbits.

The growing popularity of Indian food abroad makes it all the easier to serve afternoon coffee in the style of the subcontinent. Search local ethnic markets and delicatessens for freshly made or packaged Indian sweets and snacks, from crisp *papadums*—the lentil wafers you can fry up in a jiffy at home, following package directions—to the triangular meat or potato turnovers known as *samosas* to the sweet and subtly spiced Indian fudge known as *barfi.* For the savory treats, offer up some bottled fruit chutney to be used as a condiment. By all means, also pass around some of the fresh tropical fruit that thrives in southern India—particularly ripe, succulent mangoes. And be sure to pour freshly brewed Indian coffee.

The prevalence of ethnic Indian crafts abroad makes it all the easier to set an attractive coffee table. Spread a brightly colored Madras print or embroidered cloth. Use trays or platters, a coffee pot, and even cups and saucers of beaten brass or finely wrought silver. Other simple decorative items, too, can enhance the cultural flair of the occasion: masks or puppets, or even museum postcards or prints of exquisitely detailed Indian miniature paintings.

Don't forget some sitar music in the background—Ravi Shankar's playing is always beguiling, and you could even enhance the East-meets-West ambience by seeking out one of the recordings he made in collaboration with violinist Yehudi Menuhin.

### Gajar Barfi *(Indian Carrot Fudge)*

The natural sweetness of carrots is highlighted in this unusual, lightly spiced Indian confection.

¼ **pound unsalted butter**
½ **teaspoon ground cardamom**
¼ **teaspoon ground cinnamon**
1 **pound carrots, trimmed, peeled, and coarsely grated**
1 **pint unsweetened canned condensed milk**
½ **cup dark brown sugar**
¾ **cup coarsely chopped pistachio nuts**

In a medium saucepan, melt butter over low heat. Add cardamom and cinnamon and cook about 2 minutes.

Add carrots, raise heat to moderate, cover pan, and cook, stirring, until carrots are tender; remove lid and cook a few minutes more, stirring, until moisture evaporates.

Add milk and sugar and continue cooking and stirring until all liquid is absorbed, 10 to 15 minutes more. Stir in ½ cup pistachio nuts.

Spread mixture evenly in well-buttered 8 x 8-inch baking pan and sprinkle top with remaining pistachios. When cool, cut into 2 x 2-inch squares and remove from pan with a spatula. Makes 16 pieces.

*Traditional Indian sweets, subtly spiced, and the local coffee tempt the appetite.*

*Even in a nation as traditionally devoted to tea as Japan, coffee drinking is making inroads among cognoscenti and common folk alike.*

# Coffee in the Modern Japanese Style

Just as modern Japan has brilliantly adapted itself to and excelled in the ways of the Western world, so has coffee become a way of life to the achievement-oriented, urban Japanese. In Tokyo and other cities, a growing number of sophisticated coffee bars (one American observer of the Japanese scene counted twenty-seven coffee shops in six city blocks of Tokyo alone) brew individual cups to order, and many take pride in offering Jamaican Blue Mountain coffee—much of which finds its way there.

The Japanese yen for coffee, however, should not come as a total surprise. In fact, Japan played a significant role in coffee history. Back around the turn of the century, Dr. Sartori Kato, a Japanese chemist, was among the first to develop an instant coffee powder.

With all this attention being given to coffee, it is heartening to learn that tea has not been completely forgotten. Those who have observed firsthand how Japanese tradition still suffuses the modern lifestyle find it totally in character that a small cup of green tea is frequently served alongside the coffee itself.

That, in fact, is usually the only accompaniment to the coffee. Though coffee shops will offer some simple canape-sized sandwiches and perhaps bowls of curried rice, the Western brew is meant to be the star of the occasion, appreciated with almost Zen-like concentration.

To give the coffee its due in the Japanese coffee bar fashion, you'll need an array of individual pots and small cone-shaped coffee filters. Have several different types of beans available—including Jamaican Blue Mountain—and grind and brew each guest's coffee as he or she requests it. Then pour the coffee into either traditional Japanese ceramic cups or plain white porcelain ones whose spare design has an Asian quality to it.

You might also want to offer a selection of canned cold coffee drinks—a popular Japanese innovation that has already begun to find its way into Western countries. Blends of brewed coffee, sugar, and sometimes milk or cream, they are particularly popular with young Japanese on the go; serve them in tall, narrow glasses over ice.

Since the profusion of Japanese coffee bars seems to follow the Viennese pattern of adapting decor and ambience to the tastes of the customers, you're free to do accordingly for your own Japanese-style coffee hour. Play modern jazz as some Tokyo student hangouts do. Or put out the latest literary magazines and novels to create the ideal atmosphere for book lovers. And of course you can establish a more traditional Japanese mood if you like, playing soothing recordings of lute or flute music and hanging inspirational scroll paintings.

As with so much in modern Japan, anything goes—provided you do it properly and to the hilt.

### *Green Tea Ice Cream*

Though most Westerners would balk at sipping a cup of tea alongside a cup of coffee, ice cream flavored with green tea perfectly complements a hot cup of Jamaican Blue Mountain or other rich coffee.

**1 pint heavy cream**
**1 pint milk**
**1 cup sugar**
**¾ cup strong brewed Japanese green tea**
**10 egg yolks**

In a heavy saucepan over moderate heat, bring cream, milk, and sugar to a boil, stirring occasionally to dissolve sugar. Stir in tea and remove pan from heat.

In a large mixing bowl, whisk egg yolks until smooth. Whisking continuously, slowly pour cream mixture into bowl. Return mixture to pan and stir continuously with a wooden spoon over very low heat, taking care not to let mixture boil, until it is thick enough to coat spoon.

Remove from heat and place bottom of pan in a sink or a large bowl filled with ice. Stir until mixture is cool enough to touch. Then freeze in an ice cream freezer, following manufacturer's directions.

Makes about 1½ quarts.

Today, prayers and incense burning at a Japanese temple (opposite page) could very likely be followed by a cup of coffee at the local village shop.

A scoop of green tea ice cream (left) provides the perfect foil to a new Japanese favorite, Blue Mountain coffee.

# COFFEE SERVICES & ACCESSORIES

"*H*ow but in custom and in ceremony/ Are innocence and beauty born?" wrote
William Butler Yeats in his poem "A Prayer for My Daughter." Though the poem
expresses much broader philosophical musings, that thought is particularly apt
where coffee is concerned. The custom and ceremony surrounding coffee's service
add immeasurably to the innocence and beauty of its enjoyment. Every culture
where the beverage is loved has adapted its own table styles to the service of the
beverage, offering the modern host or hostess a literal world of possibilities for
entertaining with coffee.

# Setting the Coffee Table

An elegant and ornate silver pot and delicate china cups with silver rims. A pair of sturdy old earthenware mugs and a glass carafe. Mismatched cups, saucers, and napkins. High-tech glass mugs and a space-age plastic thermos. Finely crafted artifacts from foreign cultures.

All of these items, and more besides, have their place on the dinner table or the coffee table whenever coffee is served. And there's no great secret to deciding which ones to set out—or to go out and buy. Just let the occasion dictate what you choose. Opt for elegant, heirloom-style pieces or fine modern silver and china for more formal occasions; ethnic items when you're presenting coffee in the style of another land; beat-up favorites when the event is roll-up-your-sleeves informal. And so on.

The event at hand will also help you decide how best to present your dishware. For stand-up or informal occasions, arrange everything neatly and compactly at one end of the table or on a sideboard, allowing guests to help themselves. More formal occasions—even if the style is casual—might call for setting individual places.

However you arrange the coffee table, don't forget a full complement of plates and cutlery chosen to suit whatever you're serving alongside. Napkins in a similar style are also a must. And don't forget a sugar bowl and creamer—possibly more than one of each if your guest might require packets of artificial sweetener, or lowfat or nonfat milk.

And never forget the small touches that can do so much to make an occasion seem even more special. Fresh flowers bring the outdoors inside, and contribute a touch of springtime or summer to a winter's day. Other decorative items—from autumn leaves, seashells, rocks, and pine cones, to *objets d'art* or craftworks—add another level of interest and charm, often sparking discussion. And nothing sets a mood in quite the same way as music, played loud enough to be noticed but not so loud that it conflicts with conversation.

No great social stigma would befall you should you fail, wittingly or not, to follow any of these guidelines. Above all, obey one simple rule: do whatever you can or wish to do to make the occasion as comforting and as stimulating as coffee itself for yourself and your guests.

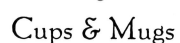

# Cups & Mugs

A remarkable collection stands on permanent display at the Los Angeles County Museum of Art. The three-decade-long obsession of Betty Asher (who once worked in the museum's modern art department and then went on to open the Asher/Faure Gallery, specializing in contemporary artworks), this collection—housed in two large glass cases—displays eighty-six beautiful, sometimes whimsical, sometimes serious, sometimes odd, and even sometimes disturbing . . . cups and mugs. Many of them are intended for or inspired by coffee.

Created by artists and craftspersons, a number of them are actually meant for use; others are more representa-

*A simple pattern of blueberries appropriately embellishes a china coffee service (page 132).*

*This fanciful mug by Belinda Gabryl is an interesting variation on a traditional theme.*

*Coffee drinking meets contemporary artisanship in two provocative collectible mugs made by George Bowes.*

tional or conceptual than functional. There's a rustic earthenware "Rock Cup" by sculptor Robert Arneson, with a solid white wisp of steam rising from its murky brown-black center; David Gilhooly's plastic "Cream in Your Coffee," in which a silhouetted cow stands in mid-cup atop an island of white cream; Kenneth Price's porcelain "Cubist Cup," oddly angled but fully functional; William Wilhelmi's "Cowboy Boot Cup," shaped as its name suggests; and Meret Oppenheim's "Objet," a cup, a saucer, and a spoon—all unsettlingly covered in fur.

If your own obsession runs in this direction, Asher's collection is a soaring inspiration. But it also provides a broader lesson to anyone interested in serving coffee: open your eyes and your mind to the many possibilities that exist for cups and mugs that might further your enjoyment of the brew. Beyond the obvious and appealing choices available in dishware departments and in kitchen

and coffee stores, look farther afield—in crafts stores, at artisans' fairs, and in souvenir shops that you might happen across. You never know when you might happen upon something that might strike a chord in your own coffee-loving heart.

More practically, many of Asher's objects also provide an important cautionary lesson: don't let beauty or some other appealing aspect of the cups and mugs you buy be the sole reason for your purchase. Pay careful attention to how comfortable and easy they are to grasp and sip from. Tiny, thin porcelain demitasses may appeal, but many a knuckle has been burnt while trying to hold a tiny handle and brushing up against the side of the cup. A cubist mug certainly has its own aesthetic merit, but grasping its angled handle and drinking from its sharp corners could well lead to more hot coffee on your clothes than in your mouth.

*Coffee pot and mugs by Stanley Mace Andersen.*

*Eye-catching and functional, this fanciful floral-based coffee pot (left) and accompanying cup (above) were designed and created by Laney K. Oxman.*

## Coffee Pots & Services

Today, informality seems to reign when it comes to serving coffee. In most homes (this author's, for one), even a formal dinner party will probably conclude with the coffee being poured from the functional glass flask into which the filter has dripped. And for most people, that suffices quite nicely.

But throughout its history, coffee has been the object of much more reverential treatment. Particularly in Europe, elaborate coffee services evolved to present the brew with proper decorum: formal or homier matching sets in silver, porcelain, or pottery, complete with tall pouring pot (into which already brewed coffee is transferred), creamer, sugar bowl, and sometimes even a tray upon which to carry it all.

If you own such a set as a family heirloom—or, perhaps, were given one as a wedding present—don't hesitate to employ it to make the occasion of offering coffee all the more special. After all, if you don't use such items, what good does it do you to have them cluttering your sideboard or hutch? A coffee service needn't impose starchy formality; look upon it, instead, as one of life's daily grace notes.

## Coffee Accoutrements & Collectibles

As with anything having to do with the social art of cooking and dining, coffee and its preparation and service have engendered a wealth of objects and ephemera worthy of the collector's attention.

Mugs and cups (see page 134) and antique coffee services (see above) are but wisps of steam above the great potful of collecting possibilities. Within the subgroup of antiques relating to the kitchen, coffee-making equipment receives a great deal of interest. The European or American coffee "biggin"—an eighteenth- and nineteenth-century form of drip-filtering apparatus, often beautifully decorated in enamel—fetches quite respectable prices. Tin and pottery pots; chrome- or nickel-plated urns; hand-cranked cast-iron grinders with glass bean receptacles; lovely wood-and-iron box mills; even old stovetop roast-

*Functional art for coffee lovers:* Something About Seeing *(opposite page), by George Bowes, and an untitled coffee pot sculpture (left) by Julianne Cline.*

*Scour any antique shop
or second-hand store
today and you're likely to
find coffee collectibles
from hand-cranked
grinders to kitchen
canisters to charmingly
labeled commercial cans.*

ers are lovely works of craftsmanship, well worthy of appreciation and display.

Printed ephemera related to coffee open up an even wider realm of delights for the collector. From old coffee advertisements and bags to beautifully designed and colored tins from earlier in this century, myriad examples await discovery at flea markets and collecting fairs the world over. And follow coffee's trail into still other realms of collecting: antique prints depicting the fine art of enjoying coffee; cartoons about coffee; sheet music for such coffee-inspired classics as "The Java Jive" and Bach's "Coffee Cantata"; coffee-themed postage stamps from nations that derive much of their livelihood from the bean. All such items are tailor-made for framing and hanging—ready to remind you (as if you needed reminding) that the time is nigh for another cup of coffee.

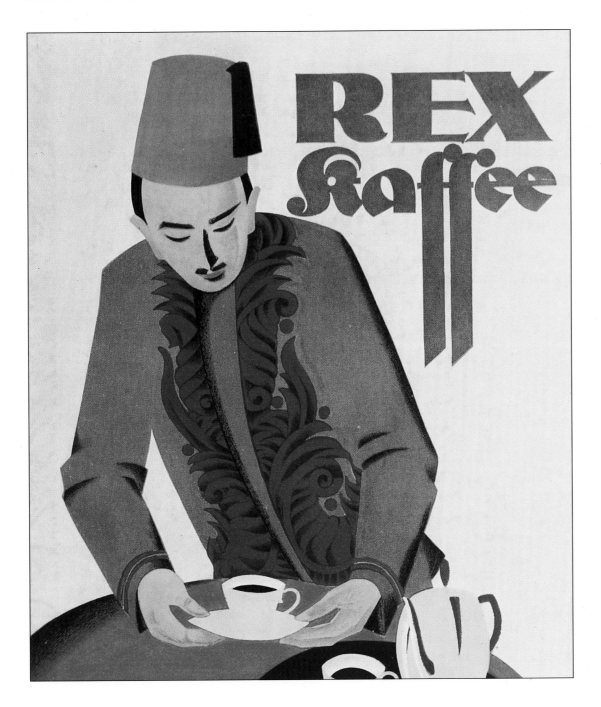

*Coffee advertising, such as this German poster (circa 1920), crosses over into the realm of fine art. Many such decades-old pieces of printed ephemera are well-suited for framing.*

# INDEX

# PHOTO CREDITS

**Principal Photographer:**
**Bill Milne**

Food Stylist: Kathy Blake

Photographs © Bill Milne pp:
Front jacket, back jacket, 54,
68–69, 71, 72–73, 76, 81, 83,
86, 89, 90, 95, 98, 103, 108,
112, 116, 120–121, 126–127,
131, 132, 136, 139, 140

Other sources include:

Stanley Mace Andersen p. 136
  (right), courtesy of the Ferrin
  Gallery, Northampton, MA
Art Resource, New York pp. 12,
  15, Joseph Martin/Scala 141
George Bowes pp. 43, 136 (left),
  139, collection of the artist
© Thomas C. Boyden, pp. 44–45
Tom Brownold pp. 30, 117
Burke/Triolo Photographic Studio
  p. 80
Julianne Cline p. 138, courtesy
  of the Ferrin Gallery,
  Northampton, MA

Betty Crowell pp. 35, 58,
  106–107
Alan Detrick p. 53
Belinda Grabryl p. 135, courtesy
  of the Ferrin Gallery,
  Northampton, MA
Dennis Galante/Envision p. 84
Frank M. Hanna/Visuals
  Unlimited p. 94
Jean Higgins/Envision p. 119
Robert Holmes p. 77
Max and Bea Hunn/Visuals
  Unlimited p. 89
Rich Iwasaki pp. 128, 130
Wolfgang Kaehler pp. 27, 31, 32,
  36–37, 46, 96
Fred Lyon pp. 8, 62, 101, 102
Michael Major/Envision p. 34
M.A. Malini/Dinodia Picture
  Agency p. 125
Larry Mellichamp/Visuals
  Unlimited p. 33
Art Montes De Ocala/FPG
  International p. 47
Rudy Muller/Envision pp. 20–21
Steven Mark Needham/Envision
  pp. 92, 114–115
North Wind Picture Archive
  pp. 17, 18, 23, 26, 33
Zeva Oelbaum p. 104

Laney K. Oxman p. 137 (both),
  courtesy of the Ferrin Gallery,
  Northampton, MA
Steve Pace/Envision pp. 56–57
Susanna Pashko/Envision pp.
  66–67, 88–89
Amy Reichman/Envision p. 56
Karlene V. Schwartz pp. 2, 6, 123
Carol Simowitz p. 10
Aravind Teki/Dinodia Picture
  Agency p. 124
Milton H. Tierney, Jr./Visuals
  Unlimited pp. 28, 110
Steve Wabble p. 11
Nancy M. Wells/Visuals Unlimited
  pp. 24–25
Robin White/FotoLex p. 39
Jules Zalon/FPG International
  p. 64

All flag illustrations © The Flag
  Research Center, Winchester,
  MA

Equipment p. 54 courtesy of
  Zabar's, New York
Ceramic tiles courtesy of Country
  Floors, New York
Dishes courtesy of
  Williams-Sonoma